# CREDIT
# SECRETS

How One Couple Beat the Odds and
Took Control of Their Credit &
Finances... And How You Can Too!

## Scott & Alison Hilton

# Refer a Friend and Get $30!

**Earn some extra money referring friends and family to the Credit Secrets Program.**

When you sign up for our referral program, you'll receive your special personalized link. Send people to the Credit Secrets website by sharing this link.

**Every time someone purchases the Credit Secrets book, you'll earn a referral fee of $30!**

**Go To: http://CreditSecrets.com/getpaid to get started now!**

# Introduction

Did you know that there are millions of errors on consumer credit reports?

There are accounts being reported incorrectly by date, spelling, name, status, age, and many other ways. Even valid accounts can be invalidated by a simple reporting error because credit bureaus, creditors, and collection agencies are held to strict federal and state laws regarding the way they report your credit. Simply challenging an item that you do not recall can also do the trick, when worded properly.

Our members have removed THOUSANDS of inquiries, late pays, charge-offs, collections, repossessions, judgments, tax liens and bankruptcies. And it happens because debt collectors, creditors, and credit bureaus are notoriously bad at keeping records, and at following the letter of the law. Even if one alphanumeric character is missing, you may have grounds for removal.

It is all about gaining leverage when a collector, a creditor, or a credit bureau is doing something wrong, and then using that as leverage for removal.

The credit bureaus must obey many laws, including the Fair Credit Reporting Act (FCRA). And according to the FCRA, an item on your report MUST be removed if it is any of the following:

1. **Inaccurate** - maybe an item isn't yours, your high balance or account number are incorrect, a closed account is listed as open (or vice versa), the date of last activity is incorrect, and so on. There are MANY other factors as well.

2. **Incomplete** - a field is blank, a number or word is truncated, a number or letter is missing, false numbers or letters are added, or something is reported in the wrong field.

3. **Unverifiable** - you may want proof that a debt collector has the right to collect from you, and you come to find out that they don't have your original hand-signed contract on file anymore - paperwork gets lost. No proof of contract means no authority to report or collect from you. Or how about a late pay - does the creditor have proof in the form of your canceled check? Doubtful.

## Did you know?

The FTC conducted a study between 2002 and 2014 that determined about 40 million people across the United States had at least one error on one of their major credit reports. These errors affected their scores and cost the consumers thousands of dollars in higher interest rates on loans and other fees based on credit history.

We will show you how to look closely at your credit reports to reveal issues that may be hidden in plain sight. There are dozens and dozens of issues to look for and several loopholes that can work in your favor.

It has been said that credit bureaus lean towards retaining incorrect data, rather than the other way around, because they profit from the more data that they have. After all, they are essentially data brokers. So more data is worth more money, even if some of it is being incorrectly reported. It has also been said that finding incorrect data on your report could be enough to scare you into buying their identity theft monitoring products, which account for over 10% of their revenue.

The most important thing to know when you are working on fixing your credit, is that you are dealing

## Top 5 Creditor Violations

1. Call you before 8am or after 9pm
2. Contact a third party such as an employer or friend for any reason other than getting contact information.
3. Lie about the amount you owe
4. Threaten to garnish or sell your property
5. Give false credit information to a credit reporting company.

with large unorganized companies. Companies that are held accountable to timelines and requirements that more often than not, they simply cannot meet. As you will learn, they have employed all sorts of interesting "automated" tactics in an attempt to deal with these deadlines. And yet, many times the computerized methods fail to do their job properly.

As you will see when you begin the process, an alarming number of these companies have likely already broken the law in numerous ways as it relates to your own credit files.

You probably have items just sitting there, waiting to be removed. The creditors, collection agencies and credit bureaus just need a gentle nudge in the right direction. And thankfully, with the information in this book, you will become an informed consumer with the law on your side. You may find that many of your negatives can be removed in a relatively short period of time.

Using strategic correspondences and timelines will allow you to flip the script, and control your own destiny. No longer will you be subject to harassing phone calls, threatening letters, or worse. Ultimately, the goal is for you to become a confident individual who can walk into a bank, a car dealership, or a mortgage broker's office KNOWING you have a 700+ credit score with impeccable credit history.

With your credit score determining what you are allowed to buy, and at what interest rate, it is time to take full control. This is serious business that should not be taken lightly.

Many readers have made mistakes in the past, and that is perfectly okay because you are NOT your past. You are whatever you decide to be from this point forward. If you will accept that mentality and follow the steps it takes to achieve it, you may find yourself joining the "700 Club" much sooner than you ever imagined possible. And you will also arm yourself with the knowledge on how to avoid making costly credit mistakes in the future.

Bianca ▶ Credit Secret
24 mins

I've had some huge #SMCWINS I started this program bc my husband and I started to lease purchase a home about 2 1/2 years ago bc we had horrible credit but wanted a house and not throw our money complete away like we've been doing. At the end of year 3, a partial of our monthly notes would accumulate a down payment to actually purchase the house...Any who, 5 creditors have deleted they're reporting to all 3 CBs!!! I have 3 more I'm working on which should be gone by the end of the month!! I have 2 credit cards and a few store cards since I've been in tis program (the end of October). I have no negative items on my Experian report my score is up 100+ points...at one point I thought I was gonna have to take one creditor to court but before I knew, it was gone. I've also been working on his, score went up 100+ too!!! the system worked faster for him, it took the second round of letters for things to change on my report, I was patient lol. We're getting credit card offers in the mail...im freaking here!!! I tell my friends and family their freaking out!!! Thanks #SMC #Scott&Allison

Love      Comment

Please be sure to join our Facebook group using the link inside your member's area. Our Facebook group is full of thousands of people who have already improved their credit scores, as well as others who are on the same journey as you. The group is private to outsiders, and the positive energy inside is contagious. On any given day you will see folks showing pictures of themselves holding the keys to their dream car or house. We've received thousands of unsolicited testimonials and we love it!

We hope to see you in the group soon, reporting back on your own achievements!

Remember, no one is too far gone to benefit from this book. We've had members with credit scores under 400, so no matter your situation, we are here to help. Whether it's a bankruptcy, charge-off, collection account, public record, tax lien, medical bill, student loan, etc - it doesn't matter... ALL of these and more can be removed if there is any funny business going on. And chances are, even if you think there isn't - there likely is. You just need to look deeper.

So with that said, let's get on with showing you how it's done!

Kelly ✎ enjoying the long weekend.
November 11, 2016

God bless this group, for the continued support from each other. Our common goal has brought us together and we have UNITED and all become stronger in knowledge , courage and confidence. We are all different colors, races , religions ,etc and it does not matter. We are the example to be followed!
I look forward everyday to reading the success of our members to keep me strong on the days when I want to give up.
We are EMPOWERED.

Like      Comment

You, Brian      and 29 others

# Important Notes

Please follow this method from start to finish, step by step. And do not skip ahead, or you risk missing a key element that could be the decisive factor in your success or failure.

## Make sure you are well organized

We recommend actual file folders, and keeping reminders on your cell phone or a calendar for very important cutoff dates. Keeping track of who got what, who replied or didn't, and when, is essential.

Your goal is to become "not worth it" for banks, credit bureaus and collectors, by showing them that you know the law AND that you are more organized than they are.

You will point out exactly how they broke the law. And they can either remove the derogatory credit they are reporting, or pay damages - or both. Fortunately, with this guide you will quickly make it known to the banks, credit _ bureaus, and collections agencies that they will find it much easier to simply remove the negative item and leave you alone.

You may want to enlist another member, or a friend or family member to help you stay accountable. It is easy to get distracted with life, and miss important action items in your credit repair process.

**PLEASE NOTE:** Our method is extremely effective and could potentially be used for "bad" by an unethical person. So before going any further, please promise that you will approach our system with INTEGRITY, and further agree that after your credit is fixed/improved, you will NOT go back into any old bad habits. If you intend to purposely defraud a bank or financial institution by making false claims or applying for a credit card or loan that you know you cannot pay back, simply because you know you can re-use our method to potentially erase the item off of your credit report again, then we have a problem with that.

We do not want the method abused or used in any potentially fraudulent way. Please only proceed if you agree.

## Your Credit Secrets Member Dashboard
The dashboard is located at **creditsecret.org/login**.

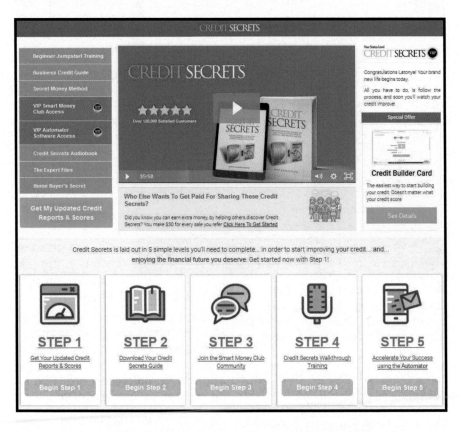

Dolores
October 15, 2016 ·

This program works! Keep the faith and god luck yo all of you who are working towards the same goal!!! Bought our first house! Huge WIN!!!

support for your journey. We also post tips and tricks that come along as time goes on.

You can request access to the Smart Money Club by visiting **https://www.facebook.com/groups/creditsecret** and submitting a join request. Many members who do not use Facebook for personal reasons, opt to create an account they only use for the group.

We highly recommend that you consider taking advantage of the Smart Money Club VIP members area, as well as the private Facebook Group.

Thousands of members have taken the road you are about to embark on, and they can offer insight and advice. Our Facebook Group is a place of no judgment, positive energy, and

If your name is different on Facebook than the name you used when you purchased our program, please contact support by emailing us at **support@creditsecret.org** and let us know so we can accept you.

As soon as you're approved, make a post introducing yourself in the

## Be sure to follow the steps ...

Credit Secrets is laid out in 5 simple levels you'll need to complete... in order to start improving your credit... and... enjoying the financial future you deserve. Get started now with Step 1!

**STEP 1**
Get Your Updated Credit Reports & Scores
Begin Step 1

**STEP 2**
Download Your Credit Secrets Guide
Begin Step 2

**STEP 3**
Join the Smart Money Club Community
Begin Step 3

**STEP 4**
Credit Secrets Walkthrough Training
Begin Step 4

**STEP 5**
Accelerate Your Success using the Automator
Begin Step 5

Facebook group along with the tag: **#Jumpstart**

We want to get to know you so we can help you on this journey! Approvals are usually very quick. While you're waiting, send out the address correction letter you just created!

Please also be sure to read our FAQ at the end of this guide. If you have a question that isn't answered there, you can submit a support ticket to: **support@creditsecret.org**

### Pro Tip: Facebook Search

Do a search inside our Facebook group for "SMCWIN" and you will find the very best posts of people sharing exactly what they did to find success with our program.

**And PLEASE...** once you have achieved success... send us an update at the HELP DESK or post it in the Facebook Group with the hashtag #SMCWIN (Smart Money Club Win). This helps to motivate others and allows you to pay it forward!

**Barbara**
November 16

One Portfolio Recovery Account DELETED from TU I have still still disputed the other one so hopefully it'll be deleted as well 😊

# #SMCWIN !!

👍 Like 💬 C

👍💙 You, Brian Ba

**LaTosha**
November 21, 2016 ·

#SMCWIN contacted CFPB for diversified consultants $453 Sprint bill and it is being deleted and all collection efforts ceased! Only 2 more collections to go!

👍 Like 💬 Comment

👍💙 You, Brian        Ebony        and 36 others

# Table of Contents

# Scott & Alison Hilton (the Authors)

Scott has been an online marketer for 15+ years.

Alison previously worked as a fashion designer and is currently a stay-at-home mom.

Together, they have 4 children and are avid dog lovers, donating their time and money to local shelters.

Both Alison and Scott have faced many trials and tribulations with personal credit. Scott first learned what would become the basis of this book several years ago after he took 13 of his creditors, collection agencies, and the credit bureaus to small claims court. He was ultimately victorious 12 of the cases.

After comparing notes with longtime friend, Jay Hannon, they tested the resulting

theories on Alison's credit report. With patience and perseverance, she ended up using the materials in this book to raise her credit score from 588 to 781 in only 90 days. (without going to court or talking to a single person)

Scott, Alison and Jay then went on to test the material with other family members and friends. Once they saw the amazing results, they knew they had been called to share this valuable, life-changing information with as many people as possible!

# Meet the Team
## (who each started out as customers first!)

I purchased Credit Secrets in 2014 because I had a terrible score in the low 500s, which made it impossible to get a credit card, business loan, car, apartment, or anything. I finally made the decision to step up and take control of my credit situation.

After diligently following this program for six months, I was able to increase my credit score to a 781! Since then, I've been able to purchase two luxury cars, personal loans, obtain seven credit cards with travel and cash reward benefits with limits as high as $50,000!

**Stefan**
**Washington, D.C.**

When the opportunity presented itself, I decided to join the Credit Secrets support team, so I can give back and help others go through the same process that worked so well for me!

Here at Credit Secrets, we are not just support reps, we are part of a mission that is much bigger than all of us. I'm here to help touch as many lives as I possibly can with this life changing information. This book has changed the lives of thousands of people and there's no reason why you can't be the next success story. If you need any assistance, send us an email or send me a quick chat message inside of the members dashboard.

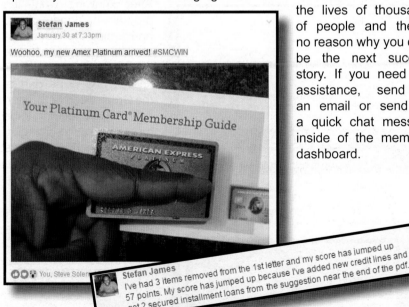

**Stefan James**
January 30 at 7:33pm

Woohoo, my new Amex Platinum arrived! #SMCWIN

Your Platinum Card® Membership Guide

AMERICAN EXPRESS

You, Steve Solem

**Stefan James**
I've had 3 items removed from the 1st letter and my score has jumped up 57 points. My score has jumped up because I've added new credit lines and got 2 secured installment loans from the suggestion near the end of the pdf.

# Meet the Team

Growing up, my parents would warn me about being careless with my financial responsibilities. Needless to say, I didn't heed their warnings and I had to learn the hard way. After a number of collections, numerous accounts with late payments and a judgment, I was stuck with a score in the low 500s with zero chance of being able to get approved for anything.

I was beyond frustrated and knew I needed to do something. As a single mom, I realized the importance of improving my credit, not only for me but for my child and our future as well. I purchased the Credit Secrets book and through this program was able to remove all my derogatory accounts including student loans and a judgment.

**Britt**
**Atlanta, GA**

I am now proud to say that I am a few points away from the 700 club (happy dance!) and have been approved for numerous credit cards! My current goal is to purchase a home and I am positive that it will be a smooth and easy process with my new credit profile, thanks to Credit Secrets.

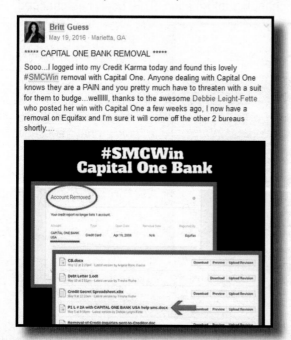

After knowing what the program has done for me and seeing the thousands of members that this program was helping, I knew I had to be part of the Credit Secrets Support Team. It's so fulfilling to be a part of this life-changing process: helping people that truly need it, as I did years ago. For anyone needing our assistance, we can be found in the member's area or at the support desk. Come say hi!

I came across Credit Secrets at a time when I was feeling hopeless. I had resigned myself to a life of poor/no credit, dodging collection calls, mounting late fees and exorbitant interest rates. I came across this program and thought to myself, "What do I have to lose?" The fact that there was also a community of people just like me sharing their experiences, questions, tips and successes was the clincher for me.

I immediately read the book from cover to cover TWICE and set about my plan with determination to change my situation and help my family and I have a better financial life.

**Leani**
**Florida**

In less than a year, I went from being someone

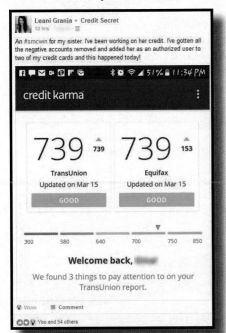

who could not get credit for anything, to having a mailbox full of credit offers daily. My scores went from bad to good to excellent. I thought this would be a daunting task, but on the contrary, it was fun like a game of elimination. It is true that cash is king, but having good credit is better!

Originally a City girl (born and raised in New York) now residing in the Sunshine State. Now that I am more financially stable, I can enjoy my four children: My Small (Isabella 3), Medium (Jaden 12), Large (Caleb 18), and XL (Steven 24). They are the lights of my life and I love spending time with them, watching them grow, and traveling around the world.

I decided to join the Credit Secrets support team to help others achieve their own goals, to give back by encouraging and supporting members who are taking their first steps in changing the rest of their lives. To celebrate with those who reach and exceed their own personal goals of buying new cars and homes, having the credit they always dreamed of, and to lovingly push those who feel overwhelmed or defeated, as I once did.

# Meet the Team

I originally purchased the Credit Secrets program in August 2015, after years of paying with cash for everything in an attempt to try to get my credit back on track.

**Steve**
**Lancaster, PA**

It took a few months before I took the time to really get started, but once I joined the Smart Money Club Facebook group and started applying what I learned from reading the book cover to cover, my scores increased the very first month. They went from 545 to 650 in a short while and I've now been able to get several major credit cards with a combined total of about $4,000 in credit.

After a few months of helping others out with their questions in the Facebook group I jumped at the chance to be a part of the Credit Secrets Support Team. I truly enjoy helping support such a great family of members! It's wonderful to get to pay it forward and help others who are just starting on their credit repair journey. I love reading the many success stories from people who were able to turn their lives around thanks to the Credit Secrets system!

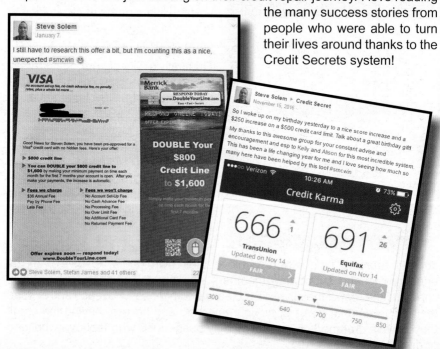

**Steve Solem**
January 7

I still have to research this offer a bit, but I'm counting this as a nice, unexpected #smcwin 😊

**VISA**
no account set-up fee, no cash advance fee, no penalty
rates, plus a whole lot more ...

**Merrick Bank**
RESPOND TODAY
www.DoubleYourLine.com
Easy • Fast • Secure

RESPOND ONLINE TODAY!
OFFER EXPIRES

Good News for Steven Solem, you have been pre-approved for a Visa® credit card with no hidden fees. Here's your offer:

▶ **$800 credit line**

▶ **You can DOUBLE your $800 credit line to $1,600** by making your minimum payment on time each month for the first 7 months your account is open. After you make your payments, the increase is automatic.

**DOUBLE Your**
**$800**
**Credit Line**
**to $1,600**

Simply make your minimum payment
on time each month for the
first 7 months

| Fees we charge | Fees we won't charge |
|---|---|
| $36 Annual Fee | No Account Set-Up Fee |
| Pay by Phone Fee | No Cash Advance Fee |
| Late Fee | No Processing Fee |
| | No Over Limit Fee |
| | No Additional Card Fee |
| | No Returned Payment Fee |

**Offer expires soon — respond today!**
www.DoubleYourLine.com

Steve Solem, Stefan James and 41 others     22

**Steve Solem** ▶ Credit Secret
November 15, 2016

So I woke up on my birthday yesterday to a nice score increase and a $250 increase on a $500 credit card limit. Talk about a great birthday gift! My thanks to this awesome group for your constant advise and encouragement and esp to Kelly and Alison for this most incredible system. This has been a life changing year for me and I love seeing how much so many here have been helped by this tool #smcwin

●●○○ Verizon 🛜                                    ◉ 73% 🔋
                    10:26 AM
                **Credit Karma**                    ⚙️

**666** ▲         **691** ▲
          1                      26
**TransUnion**          **Equifax**
Updated on Nov 14      Updated on Nov 14
FAIR ⟩                   FAIR ⟩

300        580      ▼   ▼              750    850
              640          700

I have had a roller coaster ride with my credit history over the past few dozen years. Periods of financial strain, coupled with not wanting to pay attention to it took toll on my scores. Ending up in the high 500's at one point even led me to being naive enough to pay a credit repair firm a monthly fee to fix it. It never worked, but they sure did get a lot of my hard earned money.

**Erika**
**Blairsville, GA**

I learned about the Credit Secrets program back in 2014, and signed up, knowing that a good credit score was the key to a lot of financial issues. Being self-employed since 1998, I had a really hard time building a good credit history because I would never take out any loans.

My husband and I have some life goals, and one of them was to be sure to break back into the coveted 800s. We both had items on our credit reports that weren't ours, old collections that had been paid but never removed, late payments on student loans. Even bad addresses and employers neither of us had ever worked for. We needed a new truck and the rising costs of vehicles today we needed to qualify for a loan. After digging in and getting to work, over the past year we're both cruising in the high 700's. My husband is actually almost in the 800's, and our interest rates are very low.

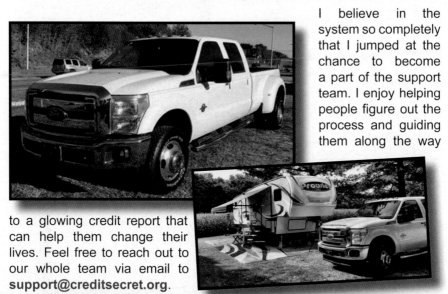

I believe in the system so completely that I jumped at the chance to become a part of the support team. I enjoy helping people figure out the process and guiding them along the way to a glowing credit report that can help them change their lives. Feel free to reach out to our whole team via email to **support@creditsecret.org**.

# Meet the Team

Jay worked at a huge, well known, collection agency for many years in Buffalo, NY, which is the epicenter of the vast and intimidating collection industry. He witnessed firsthand how many good folks were being treated unfairly and even illegally.

When he finally decided he couldn't take it anymore, he connected with Scott & Alison in order to help educate consumers on their rights. Helping others with their credit issues was a way of cleansing himself from his dark, depressing past.

**Jay**
**Somewhere, US**

Ultimately, Jay's goal is to get this book in the hands of 1 million families throughout the United States, so they can be informed and empowered to make positive changes in their lives. With so many people being torn apart by money problems, he believes this book can help to keep families and marriages together.

After all, life is stressful enough as it is!

---

**Amaya** celebrating success.
February 29 at 1:22pm ·

Look at this beautiful thing. Wow! My score went from low 600s to this amazing, almost 800 thing of beauty. And all it took was a few letters 😊 Thank you to all in this group!

| Overview | Accounts | Credit Inquiries | Collections | Public Records |
| --- | --- | --- | --- | --- |

Find basic information from your credit report on this page, including an overview of your credit score and credit accounts. You can also find personal information, such as your reported names and addresses, here.

Your Credit Score

**778**
300    Excellent    850

Account Mix

| | |
| --- | --- |
| Credit Cards | 7 |
| Real Estate | 0 |
| Auto | 1 |
| Student | 0 |
| Other Loans | 0 |
| Total Accounts | 9 |

👍 Like     💬 Comment

👍😊 You, Desmond, Tanchra, Kris and

---

**David B**
July 23 at 11:17am

Total of three collections accounts removed from the first letter. In 9 days I can send out the second batch of letters. This is great!

| | | | | |
| --- | --- | --- | --- | --- |
| SW CRDIT SYS | Jul 09, 2015 | 11 AT T UVERSE | $298 | TransUnion |
| CREDIT COLL | Jul 09, 2015 | 06 PROGRESSIVE INSURANCE COMPANY | $595 | TransUnion |
| STELLAR REC | Jul 02, 2015 | 01 DISH NETWORK | $378 | TransUnion |

👍 Like     💬 Comment

---

**Nancy**
May 13, 2014 ·

I've had 3 negatives taken OFF my credit report just with Letter #1!! YES!! Taking 2nd actions on the others now 😊

**Stefan James**
February 28 at 7:38am

The total available credit across all of my credit cards is just shy of $200,000. Debt to utilization ratio is about 3%-4%.

If your score isn't high yet, I suggest checking out the new Secret Money Method upgrade where you can obtain guaranteed credit lines of $10,000 with no credit checks.

Check it out here: https://creditsecret.org/secret-money-method...
See More

■ **Total Credit**
**$192,170.00**

**Stefan James** 😊 feeling relaxed.
December 1, 2016

In 2016, It has been so relaxing over this past year to check my credit scores knowing that I'm so close to reaching the #800Club vs 2014 when I dreaded to even look or talk about my score. I owe it all to the crew at Credit Secret! #SMCWIN

743 Very Good
FICO® Score 8 based on ... data as of 12/1/2016

772 Very Good
FICO® Score 8 based on TransUnion data as of 11/30/2014

750 Very Good
FICO® Score 8 based on Experian data as of 11/30/2014

47 Comments

report.

**#SMCWIN !!**

Inquires

**Account Removed** ⓘ

Your credit report no longer lists 1 account.

| Account | Type | Open Date | Removal Date |
|---|---|---|---|
| CAPITAL ONE | Credit Card | Aug 20, 2005 | Sep 15, 2016 |

Consider checking your full credit report for accuracy.

**Leani Granja** ▶ Credit Secret
Follow · August 3 · 🔒

Yessss!! Finally 😊

Unlike · Comment · Turn Off Notifications · Share

👍 You, Stefan James, Steven ___ and Desmond ___ like this.

Luda ___ You got a Capital One removed?!? I will be taking them to court because they won't budge!!
August 3 at 10:44am · Like 👍1

Leani Granja Luda ___ I didn't think they'd budge. They're one of the companies I had planned on taking to small claims and then I checked credit karma this morning and baam! 😊
August 3 at 10:48am · Like 👍1

Luda ___ Did you get to Part 2 of the process? Or did this happen from Part 1?
August 3 at 10:49am · Like

Leani Granja Part 1 but it took 3 letters total and I modified the last letter I sent them.
August 3 at 10:53am · Like

# Get Your Credit Reports

### Step 1. Where to Get Your 3 Credit Reports & Scores

With so many companies promising that they are the best resource for obtaining your credit reports and scores, it can be confusing.

Some offer scores, but no reports. Others offer reports, but no scores. Some use different scoring models - Vantage, FICO, proprietary, etc. And on top of that there are different versions of each, such as Vantage 3, or FICO 8.

But wait - there's more! To make matters worse, car dealerships may use FICO 7 mixed in with their own algorithm, and calculate what they call "car credit".

Other lenders may only use TransUnion, while another may only use Equifax.

You could actually pull your credit score from 5 different places and get 5 different results!

That is why some of our members use multiple services to find out their starting scores. Then you can continue to check back and see how your scores improve over time.

Here are the top 5 sources used by our members:

**http://creditsecret.org/scores**

Gives you all 3 of your credit scores and reports from TransUnion, Equifax and Experian every month - free to try. (our top choice)

**Credit Karma** - Provides 2 scores and reports at no cost in exchange for viewing advertisements.

**Credit Check Total** - Provides all 3 credit reports & scores, and is owned by Experian.

**My FICO** - Provides all 3 credit reports & scores, but is very expensive.

**Annual Credit Report** - Gives you all 3 credit reports for free, once per year, but no scores are given.

# Analyze Your Credit Reports

Now that you are armed with a copy of your credit reports, the three items we are concerned with most are:

1. **"Public Records"**
2. **"Derogatory Accounts"**
3. **"Unsatisfactory Accounts"**

All of these are bad, and in that order.

1) **Public records are the worst** – these include bankruptcies, tax liens, judgments, and other items of "public record" that anyone can see.

Typically when you have a public record, you will get inundated with letters from lawyers who promise to help you. The letters are usually from lawyers who purchased your information from the credit bureaus, in order to try to sell you their expensive services. Some will try to scare you. The more creative firms will send you letters that look hand written. They aren't. Be very careful with these folks. If you would like help from an attorney we recommend Legal Shield - **http://www.creditsecret. org/legalshield**

2) **Derogatory accounts are usually accounts that have been referred to a collection agency.** These are the really annoying people who call you, and typically break the law in the process. By law they are not allowed to call you if you tell them not to.

All they care about is money. BE CAREFUL if they want to negotiate, or if they promise you anything like removing an item in exchange for you making a payment or partial payment.

Many times they will take your money and never remove an item from your credit report. They have purchased your debt from the original creditor for pennies on the dollar, so they will try to recoup those funds, and then they'll disappear.

*Please Note:* We will tell you exactly how to deal with them later in this book.

3) **Unsatisfactory accounts are accounts that have "late pays."** A late pay is where you are (or were) 30-180 days late on a payment, but have not yet been referred to a collection agency.

Now first things first, do not get upset or emotional over what might seem like a mountain of horrible information. It is well-known that credit reports contain errors over 50% of the time. You may see items that are absolutely false. You may even see some ridiculous collection account you've never heard of, from many years ago. You will soon be able to exploit their wrongdoings to your advantage.

# A Quick Look at a Sample Credit Report

## EQUIFAX 3 in 1 Sample Credit Report

### Personal Information

**Registration Information**

| | |
|---|---|
| **Name:** | Stephen X. Smith |
| **Address:** | 123 Main Street, Anywhere, VA 12345 |
| **Social Security Number:** | 022-22-2222 |

**Identification Information**

| | Equifax | Experian | TransUnion |
|---|---|---|---|
| | Reported | Reported | Reported |
| **Name:** | JOHN Q PUBLIC | JOHN Q PUBLIC | JOHN Q PUBLIC |
| **Social Security Number:** | 022-22-2222 | 022-22-2222 | 022-22-2222 |
| **Age or Date of Birth:** | 03/1958 | 03/1958 | 03/1958 |

**Address Information**

| | Equifax | Experian | TransUnion |
|---|---|---|---|
| | Reported | Reported | Reported |
| **Address:** | 123 MAIN ST | 123 MAIN ST | 123 MAIN ST |
| | ANYWHERE, VA 22222 | ANYWHERE, VA 22222 | ANYWHERE, VA 22222 |
| **Date Reported:** | 03/1999 | 01/2002 | 10/1999 |
| | Reported | Reported | Reported |
| **Address:** | 321 EXIT ST | 321 EXIT ST | 321 EXIT ST |
| | SOMEWHERE, VA 22222 | SOMEWHERE, VA 22222 | SOMEWHERE, VA 22222 |
| **Date Reported:** | 11/1998 | 12/2001 | 09/1999 |

**Employment Information**

| | Equifax | Experian | TransUnion |
|---|---|---|---|
| | Reported | Reported | Not Reported |
| **Employer:** | ABC CORP | ABC CORP | |
| **Address:** | | | |
| **Date Reported:** | 02/2001 | 02/2001 | |

### Account Information

**American Express**

| | Equifax | Experian | TransUnion |
|---|---|---|---|
| | Reported | Reported | Reported |
| **Account Type:** | REVOLVING | REVOLVING | REVOLVING |
| **Account Number:** | 00726 | 00726 | 00726 |
| **Payment Responsibility:** | Individual | Individual | Individual |
| **Date Opened:** | 03/1991 | 03/1991 | 03/1991 |
| **Balance Date:** | 04/2002 | 04/2002 | 04/2002 |
| **Balance Amount:** | $704 | $704 | $704 |
| **Monthly Payment:** | $21 | $21 | $21 |
| **Credit Limit:** | $704 | $6416 | $704 |
| **High Balance:** | | | |
| **Account Status:** | AS AGREED | CURR ACCT | Paid as agreed |
| **Past Due Amount:** | $0 | $0 | $0 |
| **Comments:** | Charge | Charge | Charge |

**Chris** ▬▬▬

October 18, 2015

Well, it's amazing how one bureau will freely remove information while the others are stubborn as all get out. Persistence, perseverance and a tenacious reserve have gotten me an 814 FICO on Experian, no reason to quit fighting until the job is done. Time to prepare for court!!!

👍 You, Desmond ▬▬▬, Maria ▬▬ Stefan James and 9 others

Sometimes an account is only listed with one credit bureau. In the case below, a collection agency has listed the debt.

| | Equifax | TransUnion | Experian |
|---|---|---|---|
| Account Type: | | Open | |
| Account Number: | | 393XXXX | |
| Payment Responsibility: | | Individual | |
| Date Opened: | | 03/2014 | |
| Balance Date: | | 08/2015 | |
| Balance Amount: | | $2,789 | |
| Monthly Payment: | | | |
| High/Limit: | | $2,789 | |
| Account Status: | | Collection | |
| Past Due Amount: | | $0 | |
| Comments: | | COLLECTION ACCOUNT ORIGINAL CREDITOR: SONS OF ARLEY HOME IMPROVEMENT ACCT INFO DISPUTED MEETS FCRA | |

This is a medical collection showing on a single credit bureau report.

| Date Reported: Feb 15, 2017 | | | |
|---|---|---|---|
| Original Creditor Name | BERKS CREDIT & COLLECTIONS | Balance Date | Feb 15, 2017 |
| Date Assigned | Apr 28, 2014 | Account Designator Code | INDIVIDUAL_ACCOUNT |
| Original Amount Owed | $751 | Account Number | |
| Amount | $751 | Creditor Classification | Medical or Health Care |
| Status Date | Feb 15, 2017 | Last Payment Date | |
| Status | UNPAID | Date of First Delinquency | Feb 27, 2013 |

**Comments**
Consumer disputes this account information
Medical

CREDIT ABC BANK

PO Box 15847
Las Vegas , NV-891938873

**Equifax Account with Late Payment**

| Account Number: | 444459611989XXXX | Current Status: | PAYS AS AGREED |
|---|---|---|---|
| Account Owner: | Individual Account. | High Credit: | $ 20,094 |
| Type of Account : | Revolving | Credit Limit: | $ 25,000 |
| Term Duration: | | Terms Frequency: | Monthly (due every month) |

| Date Opened: | 06/21/2006 | Balance: | $ 2,078 |
|---|---|---|---|
| Date Reported: | 08/04/2016 | Amount Past Due: | |
| Date of Last Payment: | 07/2016 | Actual Payment Amount: | $ 400 |
| Scheduled Payment Amount: | $ 325 | Date of Last Activity: | 08/2016 |
| Date Major Delinquency First Reported: | | Months Reviewed: | 90 |
| Creditor Classification: | | Activity Description: | N/A |
| Charge Off Amount: | | Deferred Payment Start Date: | |
| Balloon Payment Amount: | | Balloon Payment Date: | |
| Date Closed: | | Type of Loan: | Credit Card |
| Date of First Delinquency: | APRIL 2016 | | |
| Comments: | | | |

**In derogatory status because of late payment.**

81-Month Payment History

| Year | Jan | Feb | Mar | Apr | May | Jun | Jul | Aug | Sep | Oct | Nov | Dec |
|---|---|---|---|---|---|---|---|---|---|---|---|---|
| 2016 | * | * | * | 30 | * | * | * | | | | | |

CAPITAL ONE

PO Box 30281
Salt Lake City , UT-841300281
(800) 695-6950

**Equifax Account in Good Standing**

| Account Number: | 486235268676XXXX | Current Status: | PAYS AS AGREED |
|---|---|---|---|
| Account Owner: | Individual Account. | High Credit: | $ 443 |
| Type of Account : | Revolving | Credit Limit: | $ 500 |
| Term Duration: | | Terms Frequency: | Monthly (due every month) |
| Date Opened: | 02/02/2002 | Balance: | $ 475 |
| Date Reported: | 08/27/2016 | Amount Past Due: | |
| Date of Last Payment: | 07/2016 | Actual Payment Amount: | |
| Scheduled Payment Amount: | $ 43 | Date of Last Activity: | 08/2016 |
| Date Major Delinquency First Reported: | | Months Reviewed: | 99 |
| Creditor Classification: | | Activity Description: | N/A |
| Charge Off Amount: | | Deferred Payment Start Date: | |
| Balloon Payment Amount: | | Balloon Payment Date: | |
| Date Closed: | | Type of Loan: | Credit Card |
| Date of First Delinquency: | N/A | | |
| Comments: | | | |

**Note: Incomplete Account Number**

81-Month Payment History

Not every credit bureau will list an account the same.

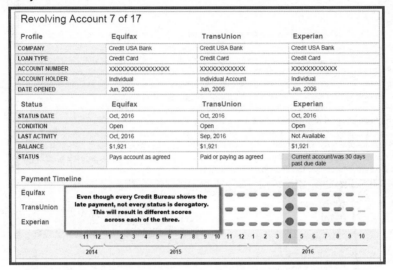

The example below shows how a payment history can be listed.

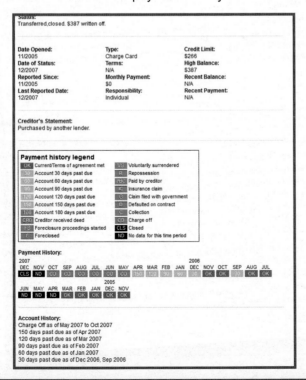

**Danielle** 🛡 feeling blessed.
6 hrs

Hey guys just wanted to update everyone. we are closing on our new home on the 31st of March that we have been building . first in November we got the preappoval and today we finally got our final Approval system auto approved chase bank pick it up .we got a 4.0 interest rate . And we are lock in and ready to go .yayaya !!! Our lender send out our appraisal guy today . Our final walk thru is the 24th and then the 31st we sign our title and pay our closing cost and we get our keys . This is the best group and program ! is so amazing 6 months ago I would of never thought we would of be able to build a house actually get approved on it , also gottten approved for any kind of credit cards, and my credit scores was 533,531,529 (when i first started ) and now my fico scores 693,675,683 . I thank everyone in is group for all the help and also for the best two people ever to come up with this program and share it with everyone . But still not finish I'm still working on a few things on my credit. I can't wait to see mine and my husband credit scores in the 700 club. Thanks again

**Dave**
6 mins

**#SMCWIN !!**

#SMCWIN

I purchased the book and joined this group back in August 2016. I had 16 derogatory accounts and 2 Tax Liens and a Chapter 7 & Chapter 13 in the Public Record which was showing on all (3) CB's when I started. I READ THE BOOK SEVERAL times. I wanted to know that book like the back of my hand.

Today there is only 1 remaining derogatory account and I just filed in Small Claims on them and I suspect once they read my complaint that will collapse like the little bitches that they are. The BK;s and TL's have all been removed except the Cpt 7 on Equifax and 1 Tax Lien on Experian.

I had great success being sued years ago in court by Debt Collectors, I was sued 5 times and won all 5 cases. I knew how to defend myself in a court against them, I was pretty much a Bad-Ass when it came to that defense.

What I knew little about was how to restore my credit. I have not applied or used credit since 2008.

A few weeks ago the Credit Secret offered how to establish $10,000.00 of unsecured credit using their method. If I remember correctly it was a (1) time fee of $69.00 upgrade for the info. Already trusting those who developed the Credit Secret book and program I did NOT hesitate to purchase the upgrade. I immediately followed the directions of that "Secret Money Method" and it WORKED LIKE A CHARM. Within 30 days I had $10,000.00 in credit and my utilization when through the roof.

I was just approved for a $25,000.00 purchase with CarMax. Im a simple guy, I don't need fancy. I love what a mini van offers.

I want to publicly thank this Team and this group for their support, wisdom, determination and willingness to fight back against those who choose to lie, cheat and do harm to people and families.

In gratitude,
Dave

# Credit Score Differences

When you start pulling your credit reports, you may find that your credit scores vary among different credit monitoring sites. So why the difference in scoring among monitoring sites and bureaus?

## Credit Bureau Score Differences

Let's first address differences amongst the bureau scores. The reason for the differing scores is due to what is actually being reported on your credit report. The credit data that comprises the reports for Experian, Equifax and TransUnion are likely different. One bureau could be reporting more negative information than the other two; for example a judgment, a collection account, late payments, etc that is not being reported to the other bureaus. Every bureau does not always report the exact same information. Additionally, a lower score could be the result of erroneous or incorrect information on your report due to human error, computer error, or even possibly identity theft in extreme cases. This is why it is critical to keep up with your report on a monthly basis.

## Credit Monitoring Site Score Differences

Understanding the difference in scores on different credit monitoring sites is very important. There are many sites online that offer credit monitoring services and/or provide your credit report (free & paid). One thing to keep in mind is that all of these sites are using different scoring systems and algorithms. Your credit scores (no matter what monitoring system you access) are calculated by the categories of payment history, utilization, length of credit history, new credit and credit mix or versatility. Different scoring algorithms place more or less weight on each of these categories causing the scores to differ.

## FICO® Scoring

The most important scores that you want to have access to are your FICO® scores. FICO® scores are the most widely used credit scores, created by the Fair Isaac Corporation. These scores are used by top lenders to help make credit related decisions that affect all of your major purchases from mortgage loans, to credit cards and everything in between. It is important to understand that not every credit score offered for sale online is a FICO® Score. In fact, many of the scores you receive online do not use the true FICO® scoring model.

Although they may not be true FICO®, they are great for monitoring your credit report itself, and to get a general idea of your scores.

 **Michael** ▮ ▮▮▮▮▮
October 24, 2016

This program is the freakin bomb

# Facts About FICO Scores

FICO scores range from 300 to 850, and they indicate whether or not you have a good credit history.

On average, any FICO score over 700 indicates that you have a good credit history.

## What Factors Into FICO Scores?

The majority of the score is calculated based on your payment history and it counts for 35% of the rating score. How much you are currently in debt accounts for 30% of that score. The length

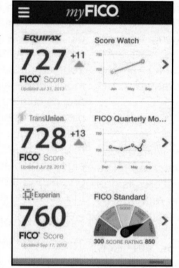

of credit history is weighed into the calculation by 15% of the calculated score. New credit and a credit mix both weigh in at 10% of the overall FICO score.

## 1. Accounts Owed

This refers to how much money you currently owe. If you have a lot of debt, it doesn't necessarily mean that you will have a lower FICO score. It does take into account the ratio of money owed in comparison to the amount of credit available. For example, if you take out a $10,000 Line of Credit, and you've extended that credit to its fullest, you will have a lower FICO score than a person who took out $100,000 but has only utilized a small portion of it.

## 2. Payment History

This is determinant on whether or not you pay your credit account bills on time. Each line of credit has scheduled payments and credit reports show whether or not payments have been late being received.

### Pro Tip: What is 30% Utilization?

Typically, credit utilization is calculated based on your total outstanding balances compared to your total credit limit across all of your cards, and lines of credit. However, some scoring models penalize you for exceeding 30% utilization on any single card or line of credit.

For example: If you have a credit card with a $1000 limit, you would try to keep the balance on it between $100-$300.

The best rule of thumb is to keep your balance below 30% on all of your cards at all times to kill two birds with one stone.

The days that appear on credit reports indicate whether you were 30, 60, 90, or 120 or more days late on payment toward those accounts.

### 3. Credit History Length

Typically, the longer a person has had credit, the better their scores. However, it is possible that someone with a shorter credit history has a better score if they have paid on time and have not maxed out all of their credit line accounts. FICO scores depend on how long your oldest account has been open as well as the age of the most recent credit line account and then considers the average overall. This is why closing old unused accounts can actually hurt your score.

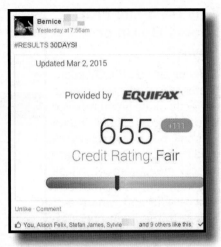

### 4. New Credit

Recently opened accounts are considered new credit. When you open several new credit accounts over a short length of time, this shows up as a potential credit risk. As a result, there is a lower FICO score. However, after some time has passed with good payment history, the score will rise.

### 5. Credit Mix

A portion of the FICO score takes into account the various types of credit accounts you have. Individuals with a good mix of credit cards, vehicle loans, mortgages, charge cards at retailers, or other financial loans will see a benefit in their FICO score.

## Why Do Some FICO Scores Go Up or Down?

Sometimes a FICO score fluctuates a bit, and that is perfectly okay. If you monitor it daily, you could make yourself go a little crazy! A credit score is not a fixed rate of measurement. It all depends on how you use your credit and when and how it is regularly updated. Your scores will also fluctuate between different Credit Score monitoring services. This is usually due to when they receive your data from the furnisher.

For example, if a credit bureau pulls your account information on the 29th of the month, and your balance

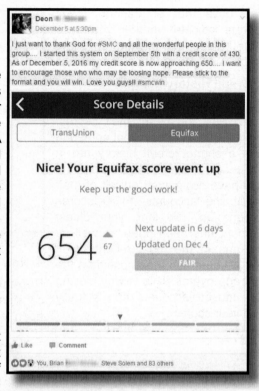

is high, and then you pay off the balance the next day on the 30th, your score will be lower than if you had paid the card off on the 28th. In that case you would have to wait up to one month to see the score benefit.

Going on a shopping spree one month and using up a lot of credit could cause a FICO score to drop. However, if spending behaviors change and less is used

on the credit account, a credit score could jump. It is recommended by financial experts that you should try to avoid carrying more than a 30 percent balance of a credit limit.

## The various models of FICO can get somewhat complicated

**FICO**
300    850

Experian, TransUnion, and Equifax already have different scores, and each version of FICO has other models. As of this writing, there are approximately 19 different scoring versions.

In 1989, FICO first introduced a scaling model that ranged a score from 300 to 850. Since then, there have been significant revisions made to the FICO scoring model which occurred in 1995, 1998, 2004, 2008 and 2014. Each year that it changed meant that a different formula was used, which also changed a FICO score. Lenders no longer use the 1995 revision, but some other lenders may still use the older versions.

The editions are named for the year they came out, and it is FICO 98, FICO 04, FICO 08 (now known as FICO 8 without the zero), and then FICO Score 9 is the model that was released in 2014.

Each has customizable versions to determine potential credit risks. If a person is looking for an auto loan, a different model may be used in the calculation of the FICO score than if insurance information was being used. These are called industry option versions, and range from 250 to 900, and are not entirely comparable to the more widely used FICO calculations.

Every credit agency uses their customized version of each FICO variation model. This is why a consumer's score may vary even when all user data is the same. The various models can become a bit confusing and unexplainable without going into significant full detail. But what a consumer needs to know is that there are different versions, and they will show different FICO scores.

*All you really need to know is that no matter what scoring model is used by a particular lender, this book is intended to help you get your score as high as possible.*

# The Credit Bureaus

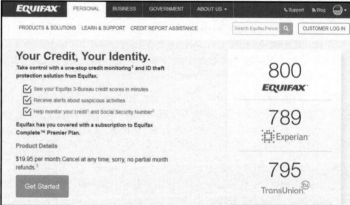

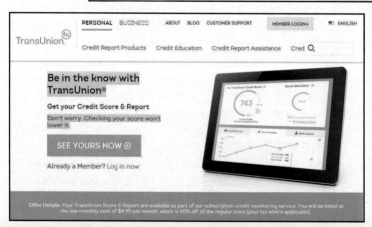

We have deliberately omitted the phone numbers and websites of each credit bureau above, because we do not recommend calling or challenging/disputing online in the beginning. We have seen the most success stories come from members who contact the bureaus by certified mail.

**STOP** *Do not contact the Credit Bureaus until you have read through this guide completely. Later on in this book we will share their phone and fax numbers for the purposes of dealing with false names, addresses, workplaces and inquiries.*

Besides, if you call it is typically very difficult to speak to someone in the USA.

Certified mail gives you documented proof of exactly when they received your letter, and then the legal clock starts ticking on them.

It is VERY important that you keep very close track of the dates as you begin this process.

Once you download your latest 3 credit reports and scores, you need to print them out. This will give you hard copies that are dated. The date will be a major factor you may be able to use against the credit bureaus to get leverage and removals.

Just keep that in mind.

The ONLY reason you will NOT succeed, is due to inaction. If you follow the guide exactly, you will do great. If not, you won't. Just do the work! It's that simple.

Experian
P.O. Box 4000
Allen, TX 75013

**EQUIFAX**

Equifax Credit Information Services, Inc.
P.O. Box 740256
Atlanta, GA 30374

TransUnion

TransUnion, LLC
P.O. Box 2000
Chester, PA 19016

### Did you know?

Postal mail is GREAT! If you file a paper tax return by mail, you are much less likely to be audited than those who e-file? – I know it's off topic, but that is something to think about – okay back to repairing your credit!

# #Jumpstart Your Success

## How to Update Personal Information on Your Credit Report

Removing old addresses and incorrect personal information such as variations of your name, social security number, birthdate, telephone numbers and employers could boost your score up dozens of points and increase the chance to remove any negative accounts associated with those old addresses.

This is a simple trick that will improve the odds of your letters working better.

Follow along and customize yours so you can send it out right away, and be on your way to your first #SMCWIN!

Look at the following image. You'll see a red circle that says "Address Identification Number". This is one of the ways the credit bureaus verify your account.

Now look further down on the second image on the next page.

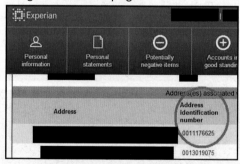

As you can clearly see, the bank has the SAME address Identification number. If there is a mismatch, you are more likely to get the derogatory

account removed.

Also, it is important to note that the entire disputing/challenging process is computerized. There are no human eyes that read your letters. In fact, your dispute/challenge letters are scanned by a computer, and a highly advanced algorithm attempts to are break it down into a two digit code through a system called e-Oscar. So if the computer notices a mismatch in the address ID, then you are also more likely to get the account removed. The same goes for your name. You may notice that your report has several versions of your name, last name first, middle initial, middle name, no middle name, etc. If you remove all of the variations, you are more likely to get the derogatory information off your report.

To update/remove change an address and other personal information, you can either mail a simple certified letter, or send a fax to one of the fax numbers below. Be sure to include a recent utility bill showing your address, as well as a copy of your driver's license and your Social Security Card.

### Equifax:
404-885-8078
888-826-0549

### TransUnion:
Complete the dispute request form and fax your request to *Attention: CCD (Consumer Contact Department)* at 610-546-4771

## Experian:

Experian no longer accepts faxes. You will have to mail in documentation for personal information changes, or use their online dispute form located at:

**https://usa.experian.com/#/registration**

A simple & free online faxing website you can use is **HelloFax.com**

If you get a busy signal, try again at another time - perhaps later in the evening.

**IMPORTANT NOTE: the credit bureaus often change their fax numbers. If you find you're having trouble getting the fax to work, we suggest using the phone call method**

to update your addresses. You may need to speak to more than one agent to get what you want, but if you are persistent, you should have no problem making this important update to your consumer record.

Here is a simple example letter you can send:

### Change of Address Letter

Date

Credit Bureau Name

Credit Bureau Address

To Whom It May Concern:

I am writing to update/correct my personal information on file with your company.

Please update my address to: [Insert Address]

Please update my name to: [Full Name]

My only social security number is: [123-45-6789]

My only and correct date of birth is: [01-01-19XX]

My only employer is: [ABC Supply Company]

I do not wish to have any telephone numbers on my report.

Please remove all the other addresses off my report, as they are not deliverable to me by the U.S. post office, and they are not reportable as per the FCRA, since they are inaccurate.

Sincerely,
Name

*Enc. Driver License, SSN Card, and Proof of Residence*

## Pro Tip: Credit Bureau Being Stubborn?

If a credit bureau is being tough and not removing any of the personal information you'd like to remove, consider going to a UPS store or any other notary. Take a bill with your current address, along with your driver's license, and get both notarized. Send this information to the bureaus and watch the old addresses disappear.

# How to Remove Inquiries from Your Credit Report

Did you know that you can remove hard inquiries from your credit report and raise your credit score? To understand how this works, first, we need to talk about the difference between a hard inquiry and a soft inquiry.

> ### Pro Tip: Soft Inquiries
>
> In general, if an online store only asks for the last 4 digits of your social security number, they are likely doing a soft inquiry. But we'll talk more later about which specific companies are best for this method.

Hard inquiries (also known as "hard pulls") appear on your credit report when a company pulls your credit report and evaluates it. This happens when you apply for new credit: a new credit card, store loan, car loan, mortgage, or personal loan. Every time you get a hard inquiry, your score can drop by a few points.

The amount of new credit inquiries account for about 10% of your credit score calculation.

That said, hard inquiries only damage your credit score temporarily. Inquiries that are over two years old don't affect your credit score and inquiries over six months old have one-half of the effect on your score compared to recent inquiries. This is why you should never apply for any new credit cards if you intend to get a major loan like a mortgage within a six month period.

A soft inquiry (also known as a "soft pull") does not damage your credit score. A soft inquiry is made on your credit report when you pull your own report.

Some companies pull a soft inquiry on your credit file to see if you're worthy of them sending you pre-approved credit card offers. Banks and other companies can also pull a soft inquiry to confirm your identity. Your prospective employer or landlord may pull a soft inquiry to assess your financial profile and risk. Credit card companies routinely perform a soft inquiry to check your credit report.

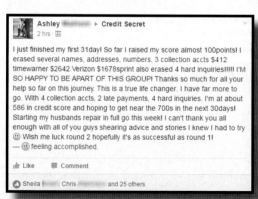

Ashley ▸ Credit Secret
2 hrs

I just finished my first 31day! So far I raised my score almost 100points! I erased several names, addresses, numbers, 3 collection accts $412 timewarner $2642 Verizon $1678sprint also erased 4 hard inquiries!!!!! I'M SO HAPPY TO BE APART OF THIS GROUP! Thanks so much for all your help so far on this journey. This is a true life changer. I have far more to go. With 4 collection accts, 2 late payments, 4 hard inquiries. I'm at about 586 in credit score and hoping to get near the 700s in the next 30days! Starting my husbands repair in full go this week! I can't thank you all enough with all of you guys shearing advice and stories I knew I had to try 😊 Wish me luck round 2 hopefully it's as successful as round 1! — 😊 feeling accomplished.

👍 Like    💬 Comment

Sheila    Chris    and 25 others

# Inquiry Removal Letters

## Inquiry Removal Letter 1

Send to the credit bureau to dispute unauthorized inquiries on your credit report.

---

Your Name
Your Address
Credit Bureau Name
Credit Bureau Address
Date
RE: Social Security Number: 000-00-0000

To Whom It May Concern,

While checking my most recent credit report, I noticed credit inquiries that I did not authorize, made by the following companies:

Inquiries:
1. (insert company name & inquiry date)
2. (insert company name & inquiry date)
3. (insert company name & inquiry date)

I did not authorize anyone employed by these companies to make any inquiry and view my credit report. This is a violation of the Fair Credit Reporting Act Section 1681b(c) and a serious breach of my privacy rights.

Please validate this information with these companies and provide me with copies of any documentation associated with these accounts bearing my signature, authorizing an inquiry. In the absence of any such documentation bearing my signature, I formally request that these fraudulent inquiries be immediately deleted from the credit file that you maintain under my Social Security number.

Please note that you have 30 days to complete this investigation, as per the Fair Credit Reporting Act section 611.

My contact information is as follows:

Your Name (printed or typed, not signed)
SSN
Address

## Inquiry Removal Letter 2

Send to the credit bureau if you receive no reply or they say the inquiries were "verified" from Inquiry Letter 1.

---

Your Name
Your Address
Credit Bureau Name
Credit Bureau Address

Date
RE: Social Security Number: 000-00-0000

To Whom It May Concern,

This letter is a follow up to my original letter dated (insert date of original letter) regarding an inaccuracy in your credit reporting. Specifically as it relates to credit inquiries that I did not authorize, made by the following companies:

Inquiries:
1. (insert company name & inquiry date)
2. (insert company name & inquiry date)
3. (insert company name & inquiry date)

I did not authorize anyone employed by these companies to make any inquiry and view my credit report. This is a violation of the Fair Credit Reporting Act Section 1681b(c) and a serious breach of my privacy rights.

I am making this final goodwill gesture to allow you to correct your erroneous reporting, and I am maintaining a careful record of my communications with you for the purpose of filing a complaint with the Consumer Financial Protection Bureau and the Attorney General's office, should you continue in your non-compliance. I further remind you that, as in Wenger v. Trans Union Corp., No. 95-6445 (C.D.Cal. Nov. 14, 1995), you may be liable for your willful non-compliance.

Failure to respond satisfactorily within 30 days of receipt of this certified letter may result in a small claims action against your company, seeking $1,000 per violation for:

1.) Defamation
2.) Negligent Enablement of Identity Fraud
3.) Violations of the Fair Credit Reporting Act

*(Inquiry removal letter #2 continued)*

My contact information is as follows:

Your Name (printed or typed, not signed)
SSN
Address

P.S. Please be aware that dependent upon your response, I may be detailing any potential issues with your company via an online public press release, including documentation of any potential small claims action.
CC: Consumer Financial Protection Bureau
CC: Attorney General's Office
CC: Better Business Bureau

**Wilfred** ☺ feeling blessed.
October 25, 2016 ·

Received this from the mail today 53 HARD INQUIRIES DELETED from experian. I have been getting some good results lately. I hope it keeps on coming.

**#SMCWIN !!**

👍 Like   💬 Comment

👍😊 You, Brian , Stefan James

**Chris** Got a letter back Chase bank( a creditor) saying that they are going to remove the item from my credit report.
January 29, 2014 at 6:07pm · Like

## Requesting the Removal of Hard Inquiries Sent Directly to Creditor

The Fair Credit Reporting Act allows only authorized inquiries to appear on the consumer credit report. You can challenge whether the inquiring creditor had proper authorization to pull your credit file. Keep a copy for your files and send the letters registered mail.

### Inquiry Removal Letter 3

Your Name
Your Address
Creditor Name
Creditor Address
Date

Re: Unauthorized Credit Inquiry

To Whom It May Concern,

I recently received a copy of my credit report. The credit report showed a credit inquiry by your company that I do not recall authorizing. I understand that you shouldn't be allowed to put an inquiry on my credit file unless I have authorized it. Please have this inquiry removed from my credit file immediately because it is making it very difficult for me to acquire credit.

I have sent this letter certified mail because I need your prompt response to this issue. Please be so kind as to forward me documentation that you've had the unauthorized inquiry removed.

If you find that I am remiss, and you do have my authorization to inquire into my credit report, then please send me proof of this. Otherwise, please note that I am reserving the right to take civil action if necessary.

Thank you,

Your Name (printed or typed, not signed)

# The Laws on Your Side When Dealing With Creditors, Collection Agencies and Credit Bureaus

There are VERY SPECIFIC laws on your side. They are hidden in between hundreds of pages of legal language.

## 1. Fair Debt Collection Practices Act

The Fair Debt Collection Practices Act (FDCPA) – this document explains the rules and laws that collection agencies are required to abide by.

Our favorite part of the FDCPA is:

*FDCPA Section 807(8) (this law is for collection agencies)*

*§ 807. False or misleading representations [15 USC 1692e]*

*(8) Communicating or threatening to communicate to any person credit information which is known or which should be known to be false, <u>including the failure to communicate that a disputed debt is disputed</u>.*

You can see the entire document here: **https://www.ftc.gov/ enforcement/rules/ rulemaking-regulatory- reform-proceedings/ fair-debt-collection-**

## 2. Fair Credit Reporting Act

The Fair Credit Reporting Act (FCRA) – this document explains the rules and laws that the credit bureaus and creditors/banks have to abide by. This is what we will refer to when dealing with Experian, TransUnion, and Equifax.

Our favorite part of the FCRA is:

*FCRA Section 623(a)(3) (this law is for creditors/banks)*

*§ 623. Responsibilities of furnishers of information to consumer reporting agencies [15 U.S.C. § 1681s-2] (a) (3) Duty to provide notice of dispute. If the completeness or accuracy*

Gene
November 7, 2016

Been at this since April. Picked up my new whip last Friday 😊 Stick with it!

👍 Like    💬 Comment

👍❤️😊 You, Alison Felix, Roderick ▓▓▓▓▓ and 160 others

*of any information furnished by any person to any consumer reporting agency is disputed to such person by a consumer, the person may not furnish the information to any consumer reporting agency without notice that such information is disputed by the consumer.*

• failure to post payments and other credits, such as returns;

• failure to send bills to your current address – provided the creditor receives your change of address, in writing, at least

You can see the entire document here: **https://www.consumer.ftc.gov/ sites/default/files/articles/pdf/pdf-0111-fair-credit-reporting-act.pdf**

Additional Laws to consider for reporting errors are:

## 3. Fair Credit Billing Act

The Fair Credit Billing Act (FCBA) - For disputes about "billing errors."

For example:

• charges that list the wrong date or amount;

• math errors;

20 days before the billing period ends; and

• charges for which you ask for an explanation or written proof of purchase along with a claimed error or request for clarification.

You can see the entire document here: **https://www.ftc.gov/sites/ default/files/fcb.pdf**

## 4. Metro 2 Compliance

Metro 2 Compliance - Standardizes the information reported to all 3 credit bureaus so that furnishers of credit information to bureaus must use the proper formatting in a form that contains 67 fields. As an example there is a field called 17a, which on your credit report would equal the section that says

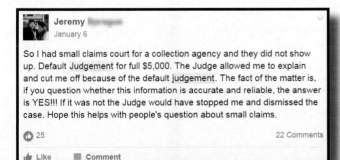

"account status". If you really want a data furnisher to be scared of you as an "informed consumer", you may reference Metro 2 when a field is missing or being reported incorrectly. and really blow their minds!

You can find out more here: **https://www.collect.org/cv11/Help/metro2formatbasesegment.html**.

And you can see where the credit bureaus settled with the Attorney General of NY, agreeing to terms of Metro 2 here: **https://ag.ny.gov/pdfs/CRA%20Agreement%20Fully%20Executed%203.8.15.pdf**

**NOTE:** If any of the above sounds confusing to you, that is totally understandable and nothing to worry about. A bit later we will tell you EXACTLY what you need to know and the steps to take.

## Dealing with Creditors

The creditor or collection agency has a right to send you letters or call you once a day, but harassing you all hours of the night, calling you at your job, or threatening you with legal action, is illegal!

Collections agencies may not use abusive language or call family members or close friends disclosing your debts to them because it is against the law.

If any of your creditors are calling you and engaging in illegal tactics, you have the right to report them to your Attorney General, the BBB and the Consumer Financial Protection Bureau. In addition, you may be awarded damages should you choose to file a small claims lawsuit against them.

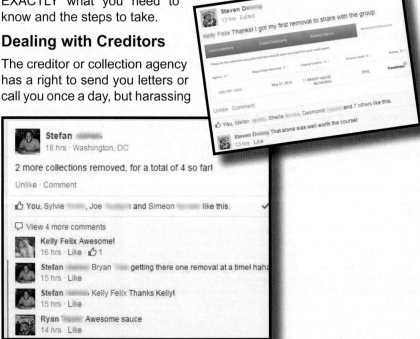

RECENT ACTIVITY

**Chris**
7 hrs

Can you say, OH MY GOODNESS, I AM SOMEBODY!

804

Your FICO® Score Powered by Experian Explanation

**Results**

We have completed the processing of your dispute(s). Here are the results:

**Credit items**

VERIZON WIRELESS                    Outcome
6709441120....                      Deleted

Visit experian.com/status to check the status of your pending disputes at any time

Unlike · Comment

👍 You, Alison Felix, Luda D_____, Erika ____ and 14 others like this.

**Chris H_____** I have a bankruptcy that has been a real bear to get removal but experience finally removed it in my score went through the roof. I just noticed this yesterday and I thought it was one of those commercial pages and when I realized it was my score I actually got tears in my eyes.
7 hrs · Unlike · 👍 10

# #SMCWIN !!

**Ebony _____** 😊 feeling happy
21 hrs

I got another account deleted

Wednesday, June 24, 2015                    Account Number: XXXX-XXXX-XXXX-63**
EBONY
P.O. BO_
N. CHARLESTON, SC. 29423

Dear Ebony Moore,

Thank you for the opportunity to serve you. This letter is in response to your recent inquiry.

We have requested that the consumer reporting agencies delete the account from your credit file.

We appreciate the opportunity to respond.

Thank you for contacting Card Services.

Thomas:
14274

P.O. Box 105555 | Atlanta, GA 30348-5555 | 1-877-846-0043 | www.mysalutecard.com

# Chapter 2: Getting Inaccurate / Incomplete / Unfair / Unverifiable Items Removed

We like to start with the FDCPA section 807(8) and FCRA section Section 623(a)(3). Remember, the FDCPA deals with collection agencies and the FCRA deals with banks/creditors.

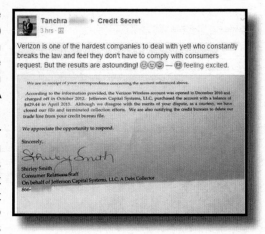

The big key item to remember is that ANY TIME you contact any of these entities questioning a line item that they placed on your credit report, they are required to contact the credit bureaus on your behalf, and make sure they add a sentence to your credit report WITHIN 30 CALENDAR DAYS that says you have disputed the negative item in question. This is because, in general, most requirements in the FDCPA have a 30 day window for resolution.

The required sentence would appear on your credit report with something like this: "Customer has disputed the validity of this item".

The thing is they almost never add the sentence. In our experience, over 90% of the time, they just don't do it.

If they do, it is usually not in time either. Sometimes they will do it within 60 days. Not Good Enough!

That's too bad for them, because by law, they MUST add the dispute notice within 30 days.

What does that mean for you?

You will get a copy of your credit report on the day they signed for your letter, and you will get another copy of your credit report exactly 31 days later.

You will then have proof that they didn't follow the law -

## Pro Tip: Keep the Oldest

If possible try to leave the oldest account open. The length of your credit history is a factor in your score. If you close that old account that you opened as a Freshman in college, that was not reporting derogatory, and only leave recent ones open, it will make it look as if you are much newer borrower.

that they didn't mark the item as disputed within 30 calendar days, and they may be liable to you for DAMAGES of up to $1,000 per occurrence. Do you think they would rather pay you $1,000 or remove the item?

This will give you massive leverage to get the items removed.

When you start the process, you will be asking the collection agencies some hard hitting questions and requesting very specific information from them.

Information such as a copy of the original contract you physically signed, supposedly agreeing to their payment terms when you opened the account.

Many companies do not have these records readily available, and in fact many have no records at all.

If you're beginning to notice, we are forcing these companies to work harder than they normally do. They usually try to collect from uninformed people who they consider "easy money" or "low hanging fruit". So we are putting them on notice that we aren't just going to lay down for them. They actually have to do their job and follow the law. What a concept!

The letters we provide apply to the majority of situations. They begin with demands for validation - i.e. proof that you owe the amount stated. They escalate depending on the response or lack of response. You should edit the letter templates to relate to your own situation and how aggressive you want to be, and what your reasoning is:

- inaccurate
- incomplete
- unfair
- unverifiable
- not yours

The letter sending process is a 2 part process.

Clancy
December 9 at 5:26am ·

Started with scores in the low 600. Closed on my dream home last Thursday. Also got approved for an American Express 10,000, PenFed 5000, Chase 5000, Walmart 2500, Hhgregg 2500, BP 2500, Sams Club 2500. I had two hospital bills on my credit when I started. I paid them off directly to the creditor. I started the program in October.

Like    Comment

You, Stefan James, Brian         and 300 others

# Part 1 Letters

**Part 1** is for dealing with the creditors and collection agencies directly.

**Part 2** is for dealing with the credit bureaus.

For best results, we do not recommend skipping ahead. The exception is "public records" (judgments, bankruptcies, liens) - for those you can skip directly to part 2, since you cannot dispute or challenge them directly with a collection agency, a creditor or a court.

## Sample Letters Templates

*IMPORTANT* – For best results we recommend sending any of the letters you use below via CERTIFIED MAIL, with a return receipt requested - you can also opt to save some money on postage by only requesting "electronic delivery confirmation" instead of getting the receipt mailed to you. Either option will not only ensure its delivery, but you will have a documented time of when it was received.

This is very important because you are going to need to prove that the credit bureaus, collection agencies, and creditors failed to properly investigate and/or mark your account as disputed within the 30 day time-frame required by law. As soon as they sign for your letter, the clock starts ticking, and you will have a receipt of when they signed for it.

On **DAY 31** (31 calendar days after they have signed for the

letter) you will print out a new copy of your credit reports, and they will be time & date stamped as well. This will provide you with proof of whether or not they marked the item "disputed" as required by the law. If they do it AFTER the 30 day mark, you now

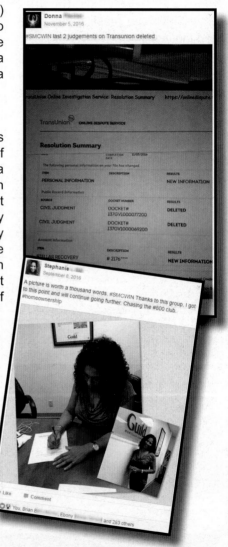

have leverage on them that they have violated the FCRA and FDCPA.

**PLEASE NOTE:** We have notes and things like "your name here" in the letter templates below. Make sure you proofread your letters and see that you've made all of the necessary edits where your own personal information is required.

According to the law, the burden of proof is on the credit bureau and/or the furnisher of the information - NOT YOU. Meaning you are allowed to challenge any item that you believe is unverifiable or inaccurate.

However, if you DO know and concede that an item is 100% yours, there are many other ways to go after remove it - instead of claiming it doesn't belong to you, you can challenge it based on any of the following potential errors that you believe may be occurring:

- Incorrect balance
- Missing information
- Incorrect credit limit
- High balance is lower than owed balance
- "Status" or any other field blank
- "Status" incorrect

- Incorrect high balance
- Late pays after an account was closed
- Account number inaccurate (may include X's or asterisks instead of full number - this is a BIG issue that we will talk about more later)
- Account type inaccurate
- Invalid furnisher (more on this later)

### Pro Tip: Dispute Anything!

It is important to note that you are legally allowed to dispute anything on your credit report because the burden of proof is on them, not you. If you do not recall an item in any way, or believe the date is wrong, the amount is wrong, or ANYTHING at all is suspicious, requesting validation is generally good practice in order to get the best and most accurate results.

- Date of last activity incorrect (the 7 year clock starts on the last payment you made, and no one is allowed to "re-age" the item to start the clock over - even paying off a collection does not reset the last payment date)
- Date of last update incorrect
- Date reported inaccurate

# Part 1 Letters

- Collection account listed with a limit, but a collection cannot have a limit

- Charge off listed as "open" or collection

While our sample letter templates below are for accounts that you claim are not yours, you should feel free to change them to the situation that applies to you, using one or more of the above issues.

Lastly, here are a few common replies you will get to the letters in Part 1 (to creditors and collection agencies):

**Blah Blah Blah**: The creditor or collection agency may reply with a letter saying a whole bunch of stuff you don't understand, and many times what they say isn't even legal or true (such as saying they don't need to give you proof of anything). We call these "stall tactics", and typically continue with the next letter.

**Verified**: The creditor or collection agency may provide you with what they call "proof", such as an itemized printout of what they claim is your account or billing statement. The FTC has issued an opinion letter on this subject, and concludes that an itemized printout does not represent verification. Here is a link to the FTC opinion letter: **http://creditsecret. org/wollmanopinion.jpg** - When you send letter #2 you will have massive leverage.

**No reply**: If they do not reply within 30 days of receiving your letter, they are in violation of the FDCPA and FCRA. You will now have massive leverage going into letter #2.

**Mail returned undeliverable** If you mailed your letter to the address of the collector/creditor that is listed on your credit report and it comes back returned, that means they are reporting inaccurate data because they provided a false address to reach them on your credit report. You can then make a copy of the returned mail and send it

Len
December 8 at 7:46pm

My last collection dropped off my TU report.. & another score increase.. 55 points this time !! ... #SMCWINNING !!! ... So grateful for that book.. Those letters.. & this group.... : ))

Your Credit Scores

Provided by **TransUnion.**

580 640 700 780

**736** ↖ 55

Good 850

Like    Comment

You, Brian Barú Murray, Leani Grania and 91 others

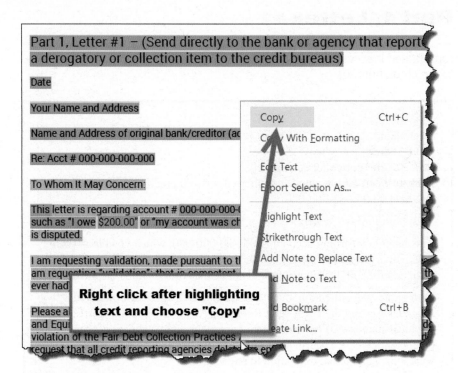

Part 1, Letter #1 – (Send directly to the bank or agency that reported a derogatory or collection item to the credit bureaus)

Date

Your Name and Address

Name and Address of original bank/creditor (a...

Re: Acct # 000-000-000-000

To Whom It May Concern:

This letter is regarding account # 000-000-000-0... such as "I owe $200.00" or "my account was ch... is disputed.

I am requesting validation, made pursuant to th... am requesting "validation"; that is competent ... ever had...

Please a... and Equi... violation of the Fair Debt Collection Practices ... request that all credit reporting agencies ...

**Right click after highlighting text and choose "Copy"**

Copy — Ctrl+C
Copy With Formatting
Edit Text
Export Selection As...
Highlight Text
Strikethrough Text
Add Note to Replace Text
Add Note to Text
Add Bookmark — Ctrl+B
Create Link...

to the credit bureaus as proof, and request removal.

## Printing the Letters

If you are reading this book as a hardcopy, you can login to your member's dashboard at **http://www.creditsecret.org/login** and download the digital version. Once you have downloaded the PDF file, you can use Adobe Acrobat or Adobe Reader to open it. Then you can simply copy and paste each letter into a word processor like Microsoft Word, Google Docs or **OpenOffice.org**.

Highlight the entire letter with your mouse and then right-click and select "Copy". Then open a new document in your editor of choice, right click and select "paste".

Then make the changes necessary to format & personalize it.

Lastly, DO NOT sign any letters you send. You do not want your signature being compared, and used against you later, if they do happen to find your original contract. A typed version of your name is enough to send the letters.

**OK enough talk - Let's do this!**

# Part 1, Letter # 1

This is the letter that you send directly to the bank or agency that reported an inaccurate, unfair, or unverifiable derogatory or collection item to the credit bureaus.

---

Date
Your Name
Your Address
Name of creditor/collection agency
Address of creditor/collection agency (from your credit report)
Re: Acct # 000-000-000-000

To Whom It May Concern:

This letter is regarding account #000-000-000-000, which you claim [insert a derogatory condition here, such as "I owe $200.00" or "my account was charged off $800"]. This is a formal notice that your claim is disputed.

I am requesting validation, made pursuant to the Fair Debt Collection Practices Act and the Fair Credit Reporting Act, along with the corresponding local state laws. Please note that I am requesting "validation"; that is competent evidence bearing my signature, showing that I have (or ever had) some contractual obligation to pay you.

Please also be aware that any negative mark found on my credit reports (including Experian, TransUnion and Equifax) from your company or any company that you represent, for a debt that I don't owe, is a violation of the FCRA & FDCPA; therefore if you cannot validate the debt, you must request that all credit reporting agencies delete the entry.

Pending the outcome of my investigation of any evidence that you submit, you are instructed to take no action that could be detrimental to any of my credit reports.

Failure to respond within 30 days of receipt of this certified letter may result in small claims legal action against your company at my local venue. I would be seeking a minimum of $1,000 in damages per violation for:

· Defamation
· Negligent Enablement of Identity Fraud
· Violation of the Fair Debt Collection Practices Act (including but not limited to Section 807-8)
· Violation of the Fair Credit Reporting Act (including but not limited to Section 623-b)

---

*(Letter continued on next page)*

*(Part 1, Letter #1 continued)*

---

Please Note: This notice is an attempt to correct your records, and any information received from you will be collected as evidence should any further action be necessary. This is a request for information only, and is not a statement, election, or waiver of status.

My contact information is as follows:

Your Name (printed not signed)
Your Address
SSN

P.S. Please be aware that dependent upon your response, I may be detailing any potential issues with your company via an online public press release, including documentation of any potential small claims action. I am also including a copy of my complaint to the organizations below:

CC: Consumer Financial Protection Bureau
CC: Attorney General's Office
CC: Better Business Bureau

---

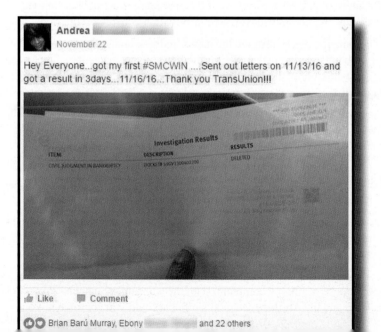

**Andrea**
November 22

Hey Everyone...got my first #SMCWIN ....Sent out letters on 11/13/16 and got a result in 3days...11/16/16...Thank you TransUnion!!!

👍 Like       💬 Comment

👍❤️ Brian Barú Murray, Ebony _____ and 22 others

# Part 1 Letter #2A

You will send this second letter only if you receive a letter back from a creditor/collection agency in reply to letter # 1, saying your account was verified as accurate.

Date
Your Name
Your Address
Name of creditor/collection agency
Address of creditor/collection agency (from your credit report)
Re: Acct # 000-000-000-000

To Whom It May Concern:

This letter is in response to your recent claim regarding account #000-000-000-000, which you claim [insert a derogatory condition here, such as "I owe $200.00" or "my account was charged off $800"].

Yet again, you have failed to provide me with a copy of any viable evidence, bearing my signature, showing the account is being reported accurately.

Be advised that the description of the procedure used to determine the accuracy and completeness of the information is hereby requested.

Additionally, please provide the name, address, and telephone number of each person who personally verified this alleged account, so that I can inquire about how they "verified" without providing any proof, bearing my signature.

As per FTC opinion letter from Attorney John F. LeFevre, you should be aware that a printout of a bill or itemized document does not constitute verification.

I am again formally requesting a copy of any documents, bearing my signature, showing that I have a legally binding contractual obligation to pay you the alleged amount.

Be aware that I am making a final goodwill attempt to have you clear up this matter. The listed item is inaccurate and incomplete, and represents a very serious error in your reporting.

I am maintaining a careful record of my communications with you for the purpose of filing a complaint with the Consumer Financial Protection Bureau and the Attorney General's office, should you continue in your

*(Part 1, Letter #2A continued)*

non-compliance of federal laws under the Fair Debt Collection Practices Act, the Fair Credit Reporting Act, and the corresponding local state laws. I further remind you that you may be liable for your willful non-compliance.

Failure on your behalf to provide a copy of any alleged contract or other instrument bearing my signature may result in a small claims action against your company. I would be seeking a minimum of $1,000 in damages per violation for:

· Defamation
· Negligent Enablement of Identity Fraud
· Violation of the Fair Debt Collection Practices Act (including but not limited to Section 807-8)
· Violation of the Fair Credit Reporting Act (including but not limited to Section 623-b)

You will be required to appear in a court venue local to me, in order to formally defend yourself. My contact information is as follows:

Your Name (printed not signed)
Your Address
SSN

P.S. Please be aware that dependent upon your response, I may be detailing any potential issues with your company via an online public press release, including documentation of any potential small claims action.

CC: Consumer Financial Protection Bureau
CC: Attorney General's Office
CC: Better Business Bureau

Dave ███████ uploaded a file.
December 4, 2016 at 5:42pm

2 Tax Liens GONE!! 😃
#SMCWIN

Liens_Deleted.pdf · version 1
Portable Document Format
Download   Preview

👍 Like    💬 Comment

You, Brian Barú Murray, Steve Solem and 53 others

# Part 1, Letter #2B

You will send this second letter ONLY if you DO NOT hear back from the creditor/collection agency in reply to letter #1.

---

Date
Your Name
Your Address
Name of creditor/collection agency
Address of creditor/collection agency (from your credit report)
Re: Acct # 000-000-000-000

To Whom It May Concern:

This letter is in response to your recent claim regarding account #000-000-000-000, which you claim [insert a derogatory condition here, such as "I owe $200.00" or "my account was charged off $800"].

By not replying in a timely manner to my initial letter on [insert date], you have not only violated federal and state laws, but you have also failed to provide me with a copy of any viable evidence, bearing my signature, showing the account is being reported accurately.

Be aware that I am making a final goodwill attempt to have you clear up this matter. The listed item is entirely inaccurate and incomplete, and represents a very serious error in your reporting.

I am maintaining a careful record of my communications with you for the purpose of filing a complaint with the Consumer Financial Protection Bureau and the Attorney General's office, should you continue in your non-compliance of federal laws under the Fair Debt Collection Practices Act, the Fair Credit Reporting Act, and the corresponding local state laws. I further remind you that you may be liable for your willful non-compliance.

Failure on your behalf to provide a copy of any alleged contract or other instrument bearing my signature may result in a small claims action against your company.

I would be seeking a minimum of $1,000 in damages per violation for:

· Defamation
· Negligent Enablement of Identity Fraud

---

*(Letter continued on next page)*

*(Part 1, Letter #2B continued)*

· Violation of the Fair Debt Collection Practices Act (including but not limited to Section 807-8)

· Violation of the Fair Credit Reporting Act (including but not limited to Section 623-b)

You would be required to appear in a court venue local to me, in order to formally defend yourself. My contact information is as follows:

Your Name (printed not signed)
Your Address
SSN

P.S. Please be aware that dependent upon your response, I may be detailing any potential issues with your company via an online public press release, including documentation of any potential small claims action.

CC: Consumer Financial Protection Bureau
CC: Attorney General's Office
CC: Better Business Bureau

# Part 1, Letter #3

This letter only gets sent if your creditor/collection agency responds with what they consider "proof" of your original signature and obligation to pay. You must wait until the 31st day from when they received your first letter, then check your credit report to make sure they have not marked the item as "disputed". If it is not marked as "disputed" in the comment section, we typically proceed ahead and send Part 1 Letter 3. If it IS marked as disputed, then you can proceed with Part 1 Letter 4 or Part 2 Letter 1 - it is your choice.

---

Date
Your Name
Your Address
Name of creditor/collection agency
Address of creditor/collection agency (from your credit report)
Re: Acct # 000-000-000-000

To Whom It May Concern:

Upon further investigation, I have retained new copies of my credit reports, and noticed that you did not furnish the credit bureaus with the required disclosure, within the period required by law. You are required by federal law to place a "notice of dispute" on my account within 30 days of my dispute, which you signed for on [insert date]. I have retained a copy of your signature and date of receipt, as well as a time-stamped copy of my credit reports, showing that you have violated the Fair Credit Reporting Act, Section 623(a)(3) and/or the Fair Debt Collection Practices Act Section 807(8) by not placing the disclosure within the required 30-day period.

Be aware that I am making a final goodwill attempt to have you clear up this matter. The listed item is entirely inaccurate and incomplete, and represents a very serious error in your reporting.

I am maintaining a careful record of my communications with you for the purpose of filing a complaint with the Consumer Financial Protection Bureau and the Attorney General's office, should you continue in your non-compliance of federal laws under the Fair Credit Reporting Act.

I further remind you that you may be liable for your willful non-compliance, as per FCRA 623(a)(3) - Responsibilities of furnishers of

---

*(Letter continued on next page)*

*(Part 1, Letter #3 continued)*

information to consumer reporting agencies [15 U.S.C. 1681s-2]

*(3) Duty to provide notice of dispute. If the completeness or accuracy of any information furnished by any person to any consumer reporting agency is disputed to such person by a consumer, the person may not furnish the information to any consumer reporting agency without notice that such information is disputed by the consumer.*

*(B) Time of Notice (I) The notice required under subparagraph (A) shall be provided to the customer prior to, or no later than 30 days after, furnishing the negative information to a consumer reporting agency described in section 603(p).*

As you have violated federal law, by not properly providing the credit bureaus with proper notice within the required timeframe, and I have evidence of such, via certified mail receipts, you must now remove the item. Any other action (or inaction) on your behalf may result in a small claims action against your company.

I would be seeking a minimum of $1,000 in damages per violation for:

· Defamation
· Negligent Enablement of Identity Fraud
· Violation of the Fair Debt Collection Practices Act (including but not limited to Section 807-8)
· Violation of the Fair Credit Reporting Act (including but not limited to Section 623-a-3)

You will be required to appear in a court venue local to me, in order to formally defend yourself. My contact information is as follows:

Your Name (printed not signed)
Your Address
SSN

P.S. Please be aware that dependent upon your response, I may be detailing any potential issues with your company via an online public press release, including documentation of any potential small claims action.

CC: Consumer Financial Protection Bureau
CC: Attorney General's Office
CC: Better Business Bureau

# Part 1, Letter # 4

You can send this letter if you have not heard back from the creditor, OR if they continue to "verify" the item without sufficient proof. This letter is for when you have taken legal action in small claims court. If you prefer not to go that route, it is completely up to you - you may want to skip ahead to Part 2, Letter 1 in lieu of filing a small claims lawsuit.

---

Date
Your Name
Your Address
Name of creditor/collection agency
Address of creditor/collection agency (from your credit report)
Re: Acct # 000-000-000-000

To Whom It May Concern:

This letter is in response to your recent claim regarding account #000-000-000-000, which you claim [insert a derogatory condition here, such as "I owe $200.00" or "my account was charged off $800"].

Yet again, you have failed to: (choose which apply)

Provide me with a copy of any viable evidence bearing my signature.

Mark the item as disputed on my credit reports

Given that I believe you are acting in bad faith, and have not complied with the federal and state laws, I have filed a Small Claims lawsuit against you. (see attached lawsuit)

I have maintained careful records of your actions, and you are now required to appear at:

(insert courthouse and address) on (insert date).

I am seeking (insert dollar amount) in damages for: (choose which laws to include depending on whether or not they provided you with evidence or failed to mark as disputed)

· Violation of the Fair Debt Collection Practices Act (including but not limited to Section 807-8)
· Violation of the Fair Credit Reporting Act (including but not limited to

---

*(Letter continued on next page)*

*(Part 1, Letter #4 continued)*

Section 623-a-3)

· Violation of (insert corresponding state laws here if desired)

Prior to our court date on (insert date) if you should decide to correct your records and remove the negative and false item in question, please contact me at the address below, and I will subsequently withdraw the lawsuit.

My contact information is as follows:

Your Name (printed not signed)
Your Address
SSN

CC: Consumer Financial Protection Bureau
CC: Attorney General's Office
CC: Better Business Bureau

**Scott**
November 11, 2016

Oh forgot to shout out my win....Ive piggybacked of my wifes good credit with 2 credit cards from capitalone...i joined the app creditwise they offer..monitoring service...well yesterday i get pre-qualified offer in mail ...says cant hurt credit score...i type in qualifing codes etc....60 seconds later.....you have been approved for 3k credit line...wow..im pumped...on my way baby....this program works this past august i was 530 fico 14 collection accounts 1 repo and 1 judgement...fico tu is 702 eq 680 ex696 have 1 collection acct left on tu/ex and 4 on eq pumped this group helped the most

👍 Like     💬 Comment

👍❤ You, Brian Barú Murray,

**Jo**
July 7, 2016

Hi to my Credit Secret family, Awesome news!!!! Preapproved for a mortgage up to $325,000!!!!! Thank you Jesus

👍 Like     💬 Comment

👍❤😮 You, Alison Felix, Jeff          and 430 others

# Pro Tip: The Automator

Are you in a hurry? Don't want to deal with copy and pasting and formatting letters in a word processor? Do you just want to click a few buttons and have your letters generated and sent through your computer via an online certified mail service?

**Have no fear!**
**The Automator is here!**

Available as an upgrade from your Credit Secrets Membership dashboard, The Automator is a PDF generator on steroids. You input a few simple items and it generates the letters for you. Once you are finished, it can even send the letters FOR YOU.

Our members that use the Automator say that it's a huge time saver especially if you have a lot of letters to send.

**Letters Created by Automator:**

**PART 1: Letters Directly to Creditors and/or Collection Agencies**

**Part 1 – Letter 1** (Send directly to the bank or agency that reported a derogatory/erroneous or collection item to the credit bureaus)

**Part 1 – Letter 2a** (Send this letter only if you receive a letter back from a creditor in reply to letter # 1, saying your account was verified as "legitimate")

**Part 1 – Letter 2b** (Send this letter only if you do not hear back from the creditor in reply to letter #1)

**Part 1 – Letter 3** (This letter is more aggressive. You can send this if you want to skip letters #2a or 2b and go hard on removal, or you can be nicer and wait to see what happens after sending letter #2a or 2b – it is

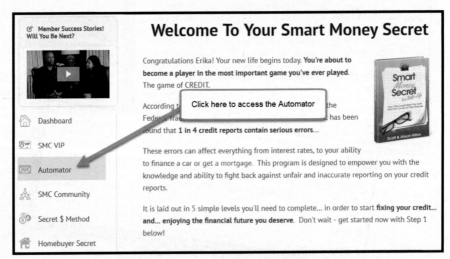

When you upgrade to the Automator, you will be able to access it from within your membership dashboard.

up to you. IMPORTANT: At minimum you must wait until 31 days after letter #1 was delivered and signed for, and then you must verify that they have not marked the disputed item as "disputed" on your credit reports)

**Part 1 – Letter 4** (Send this settlement letter if the creditor is not complying and you have filed a small claims lawsuit)

**PART 2: Letters Directly to Credit Bureaus**

**Part 2 – Letter 1** (This is your original dispute with the credit bureaus directly – Send this if you have not had success with the letters in Part 1)

**Part 2 – Letter 2a** (Send this if you

receive a letter back from the credit bureau, saying your account was verified as "legitimate")

**Part 2 – Letter 2b** (Send this letter to the credit bureau if you do not get any response from letter #1)

**Part 2 – Letter 3** (Send if you have not heard back from the credit bureau, or if they have continued to "verify" the item without proof)

**PART 3: Additional Bonus Letters**

**5 Day Reinsertion Letter**
**Goodwill Letter**
**Inquiry Removal Letter 1**
**Inquiry Removal Letter 2**
**Inquiry Removal Letter 3**
**Returned Mail Letter**
**Alternative / Bizarre Letter**
**Repo Letter 1**
**Repo Letter 2**

After you choose "Automator" from the left hand side menu, if you have purchased the upgrade you will see the big green ACTIVATED status.

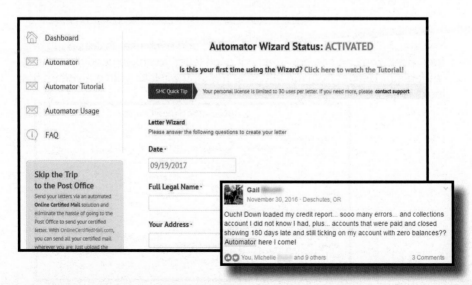

# Pro Tip: The Automator

On the left hand menu and at the top of this screen, is a link to the
Automator Tutorial.

If you have never
used the Automator
before, please watch
the entire video.

You start with a credit of 30 uses per letter, and each user is entitled to one
free reset. You can see how many of each letter you have used by clicking
"Automator Usage" from the left hand menu. It will take you to a screen that
looks like this:

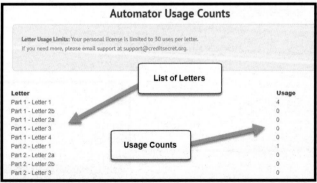

To get started filing out a letter, click "automator" fromm the left hand menu. you wil be taken to a form to fill out.

Anwer all required questions.

Choose whether you are sending the letter to the Creditor or the Credit Bureau.

New questions will open up.

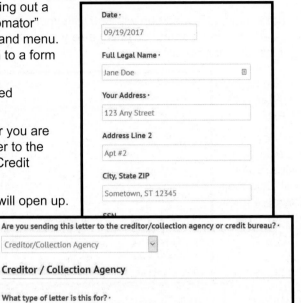

Answer each one, until you get to the bottom of the form and press submit.

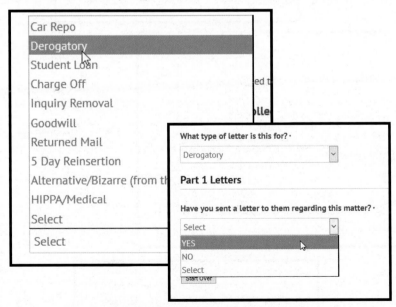

# Pro Tip: The Automator

After you hot submit, a new screen will load with your letter in an editor, where you can fine tune it or add anything else you might need, such as more inquiries, or creditors, etc.

Once you are happy with your letter, click CREATE PDF.

A dialogue box will open and ask you to save the file. Some people will have their browsers setup to automatically save to their downloads folder.

Then you can click RETURN TO LETTER WIZARD and create another letter.

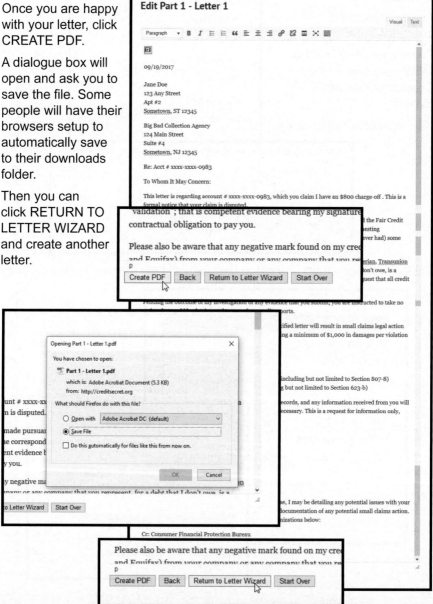

## Skip the Trip
## to the Post Office

Send your letters via an automated **Online Certified Mail** solution and eliminate the hassle of going to the Post Office to send your certified letter. With OnlineCertifiedMail.com, you can send all your certified mail wherever you are. Just upload the PDF letters you create using the **Automator**, and away they go!

Click To Get Started After You Create Your PDFs

**Get Started Now!**

If you don't have time to go to the post office, then you can take advantage of Online Certified Mail by clicking the link in the left hand sidebar.

It will take you to a service provider that will handle the rest for you. Just fill out all your information, upload your documents, and away they go!

# Part 2 Letters

Part 2 deals with contacting the credit bureaus directly. Here the focus is on something called "method of verification".

First you dispute the inaccurate, unverifiable or unfair item as per FCRA section 611(a)(1)(A).

If you get a response to your challenge/dispute from the credit reporting agency saying the disputed item was "verified"

you have the right to request the "method of verification" under the FCRA, Section 611 (a)(6) and (7). The credit reporting agency must give you the method of verification information within 15 days of your request.

This is something they typically cannot do, because they don't actually speak to anyone in order to get verification. Like we mentioned before, It is all automated through a computer, and computers make errors. A third party database was likely used to "verify" the disputed item automatically, which is insufficient. So we then request evidence such as the name, address and telephone number of anyone from the original creditor they contacted, and escalate from there.

## Pro Tip: Send Evidence

If one bureau removes an item and the others don't, or if you send a letter that gets returned, you can send either of those to the credit bureaus as evidence that they need to remove the derogatory item in question.

# Part 2, Letter #1

This is your Original Dispute or Challenge with the Credit Bureaus directly. We only recommend sending these if you have not had any success with the letters in Part 1, or if you are disputing a public record.

---

Your Name
Your Address
Credit Bureau Name
Credit Bureau Address
Date
RE: Social Security Number: 000-00-0000

To Whom It May Concern:

I have recently been informed that there is negative information reported by [insert name of collection agency, creditor or court] in the file you maintain under my Social Security number. Upon reviewing a copy of my credit report, I see an entry listing [insert a derogatory condition here, such as "I owe $200.00" or "my account was charged off $800"] in [month/year].

I challenge the accuracy, compliance and reportability of this listing.

Please validate this information with [name of creditor, collection agency, or court] and provide me with copies of any documentation associated with this account, bearing my signature. In the absence of any such documentation bearing my signature, I formally request that this information be immediately deleted from the credit file you maintain under my Social Security number.

Please note that you have 30 days to complete this investigation, as per the Fair Credit Reporting Act Section 611(a)(1)(A), and I am keeping careful record of your actions, including your Method of Verification. I do not consent to e-Oscar or any means of automated verification.

Failure to respond satisfactorily within 30 days of receipt of this certified letter may result in a small claims action against your company, seeking $1,000 per violation for:

1.) Defamation
2.) Negligent Enablement of Identity Fraud
3.) Violations of the Fair Credit Reporting Act

*(Part 2, Letter #1 continued)*

> My contact information is as follows:
>
> Your Name (printed or typed, not signed)
> SSN
> Address
>
> P.S. Please be aware that dependent upon your response, I may be detailing any potential issues with your company via an online public <u>press release</u>, including documentation of any potential small claims action.
>
> Cc: Consumer Financial Protection Bureau
> Cc: Attorney General's Office
> Cc: Better Business Bureau

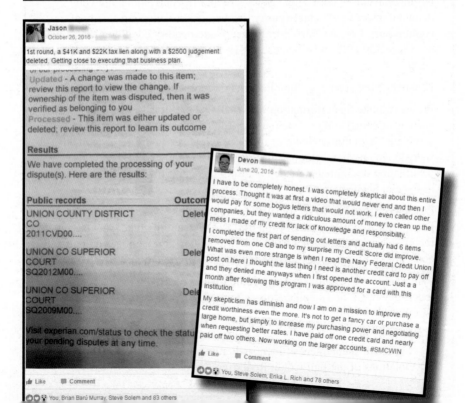

**Jason** [redacted]
October 26, 2016 · [redacted]

1st round, a $41K and $22K tax lien along with a $2500 judgement deleted. Getting close to executing that business plan.

Updated - A change was made to this item; review this report to view the change. If ownership of the item was disputed, then it was verified as belonging to you
Processed - This item was either updated or deleted; review this report to learn its outcome

**Results**

We have completed the processing of your dispute(s). Here are the results:

| Public records | Outcome |
| --- | --- |
| UNION COUNTY DISTRICT CO 2011CVD00.... | Delete |
| UNION CO SUPERIOR COURT SQ2012M00.... | Delete |
| UNION CO SUPERIOR COURT SQ2009M00.... | Delete |

Visit experian.com/status to check the statu[s] [of] your pending disputes at any time.

Like    Comment

You, Brian Banú Murray, Steve Solem and 83 others

**Devon** [redacted]
June 20, 2016 · [redacted]

I have to be completely honest. I was completely skeptical about this entire process. Thought it was at first a video that would never end and then I would pay for some bogus letters that would not work. I even called other companies, but they wanted a ridiculous amount of money to clean up the mess I made of my credit for lack of knowledge and responsibility.

I completed the first part of sending out letters and actually had 6 items removed from one CB and to my surprise my Credit Score did improve. What was even more strange is when I read the Navy Federal Credit Union post on here I thought the last thing I need is another credit card to pay off and they denied me anyways when I first opened the account. Just a a month after following this program I was approved for a card with this institution.

My skepticism has diminish and now I am on a mission to improve my credit worthiness even the more. It's not to get a fancy car or purchase a large home, but simply to increase my purchasing power and negotiating when requesting better rates. I have paid off one credit card and nearly paid off two others. Now working on the larger accounts. #SMCWIN

Like    Comment

You, Steve Solem, Erika L. Rich and 78 others

# Part 2, Letter #2A

You can send this letter if you receive a letter back from the credit bureau, saying your account was "verified" as accurate.

---

Your Name
Your Address
Credit Bureau Name
Credit Bureau Address
Date
RE: Social Security Number: 000-00-0000

To Whom It May Concern:

This letter is in response to your recent claim that [insert name of creditor, collection agency, or court] has verified that the account they are reporting under my name is accurate.

Be advised that the description of the procedure used to determine the accuracy and completeness of the information is hereby requested, to be provided within fifteen (15) days of the completion of your re-investigation.

Additionally, please provide the name, address, and telephone number of each person contacted regarding this alleged account. I am formally requesting a copy of any documents provided bearing my signature, showing that I have a legally binding contractual obligation to pay them the exact amount claimed.

Any automated response or e-Oscar verification is unacceptable. I am requesting a reinvestigation AND your <u>Method of Verification</u>.

Be aware that I am making a final goodwill attempt to have you clear up this matter. The listed item is entirely inaccurate and incomplete, and represents a very serious error in your reporting.

I am maintaining a careful record of my communications with you for the purpose of filing a complaint with the Consumer Financial Protection Bureau and the Attorney General's office, should you continue in your non-compliance. I further remind you that, as in Wenger v. Trans Union Corp., No. 95-6445 (C.D.Cal. Nov. 14, 1995), you may be liable for your willful

---

*(Letter continued on next page)*

*(Part 2, Letter #2A continued)*

non-compliance.

Failure to respond satisfactorily within 30 days of receipt of this certified letter may result in a small claims action against your company, seeking $1,000 per violation for:

1.) Defamation
2.) Negligent Enablement of Identity Fraud
3.) Violations of the Fair Credit Reporting Act

My contact information is as follows:

Your Name (printed or typed, not signed)
SSN
Address

P.S. Please be aware that dependent upon your response, I may be detailing any potential issues with your company via an online public press release, including documentation of any potential small claims action.

Cc: Consumer Financial Protection Bureau
Cc: Attorney General's Office
Cc: Better Business Bureau

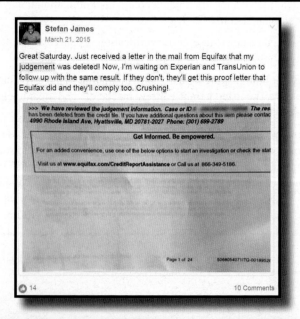

Stefan James
March 21, 2015

Great Saturday. Just received a letter in the mail from Equifax that my judgement was deleted! Now, I'm waiting on Experian and TransUnion to follow up with the same result. If they don't, they'll get this proof letter that Equifax did and they'll comply too. Crushing!

>>> We have reviewed the judgement information. Case or ID _____ The res
has been deleted from the credit file. If you have additional questions about this item please contac
4990 Rhode Island Ave, Hyattsville, MD 20781-2027 Phone: (301) 699-2789

Get Informed. Be empowered.

For an added convenience, use one of the below options to start an investigation or check the stat

Visit us at www.equifax.com/CreditReportAssistance or Call us at 866-349-5186.

Page 1 of 24              5068054071ITG-0018952

14                                    10 Comments

# Part 2, Letter #2B

You can send this letter to the credit bureau if you do not get any response from Letter #1

---

Your Name
Your Address
Credit Bureau Name
Credit Bureau Address
Date
RE: Social Security Number: 000-00-0000

To Whom It May Concern:

This letter is a follow up to my original letter dated [insert date of original letter] regarding an inaccuracy in your credit reporting, regarding the entry being reported under [insert name of creditor, collection agency, or court].

By not replying in a timely manner to my initial letter on you have not only violated federal law, but you have also failed to provide me with a copy of any viable evidence, bearing my signature, showing the account is being reported accurately.

Be aware that I am making a final goodwill attempt to have you clear up this matter. The listed item is entirely inaccurate and incomplete, and represents a very serious error in your reporting.

I am maintaining a careful record of my communications with you for the purpose of filing a complaint with the Consumer Financial Protection Bureau and the Attorney General's office, should you continue in your non-compliance. I further remind you that, as in Wenger v. Trans Union Corp., No. 95-6445 (C.D.Cal. Nov. 14, 1995), you may be liable for your willful non-compliance.

As you have now violated federal law, by not properly investigating within the required timeframe, and I have evidence of such, via certified mail receipts, you must now remove the item. Any other action (or inaction) on your behalf may result in a small claims action against your company.

I would be seeking $1,000 per violation for:

1.) Defamation
2.) Negligent Enablement of Identity Fraud
3.) Violations of the Fair Credit Reporting Act

*(Part 2, Letter #2B continued)*

My contact information is as follows:

Your Name (printed or typed, not signed)
SSN
Address

P.S. Please be aware that dependent upon your response, I may be detailing any potential issues with your company via an online public press release, including documentation of any potential small claims action.

Cc: Consumer Financial Protection Bureau
Cc: Attorney General's Office
Cc: Better Business Bureau

**Chris**
June 5, 2016

Whooo wooo!!! This surprised me today. I faxed the IRS about a federal lien. It had been released and they withdrew it. I have 2 state liens that are released. Two of the credit unions deleted all 3 but I am having trouble with Transunion. I know this update is from Credit Karma but I am still excited bout the fact that my score went up almost 100 points!!!!! #smcwin

👍 Like    💬 Comment

You, Alison Felix, Stefan James

**Trey**
July 5, 2016

Sent out letters June 14th..... Hasn't even been a month but I've had over 6k in hospital collections taking off and a 36k tax lien removed. Patiently waiting for Day 31 to approach 😃. I'm thankful for this program!!! Be encouraged... Awesome program! #SMCWIN

👍 Like    💬 Comment

You, Stefan James, Steve Solem and 92 others

# Part 2, Letter #3

You can send if you have not heard back from the credit bureau, or if they have continued to "verify" the item without proof, and you are ready to take legal action. (or you could skip ahead to the "bizarre letter" or the "incomplete/missing info letter" in lieu of legal action)

Your Name
Your Address
Credit Bureau Name
Credit Bureau Address
Date
RE: Social Security Number: 000-00-0000

To Whom It May Concern:

This letter is my final communication in regarding the inaccurate entry being reported under [insert name of creditor, collection agency, or court].

I have repeatedly asked for evidence to support your reporting, but yet again, you have failed to provide me with a copy of any viable evidence submitted by [insert name of creditor, collection agency, or court] substantiating their claims. Furthermore, I have requested your method of verification, and you have not complied, which is an additional violation of the Fair Credit Reporting Act 611(a)(7).

Given that I believe you are acting in bad faith, and have not complied with the Fair Credit Reporting Act, I have filed a Small Claims lawsuit against you. (see attached lawsuit)

I have maintained careful records of your actions, and you are now required to appear at:

[insert courthouse and address] on [insert date].

I am seeking [insert dollar amount] in damages for:

· Violations of the Fair Credit Reporting Act - including but not limited to Section 611

· Violations of [insert any corresponding state laws if you desire]

Prior to our court date on [insert date] if you should decide to correct your records and remove the negative and false item in question, please contact me at the address below, and I will subsequently withdraw the lawsuit.

My contact information is as follows:

Your Name (printed or typed, not signed)
SSN
Address

Cc: Consumer Financial Protection Bureau
Cc: Attorney General's Office
Cc: Better Business Bureau

# Public Records, Filing Complaints, and Additional Types of Letters

Public records are extremely damaging to your credit score. They consist mostly of tax liens, bankruptcies, judgments, and repossessions. Basically anything where a court was involved.

## Tax liens

The IRS defines a tax lien as "the government's legal claim against your property when you neglect or fail to pay a tax debt."

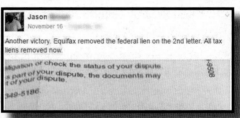

What does this mean to you? It means the government has the right to take your property away from you and either sell it or keep it to satisfy your unpaid taxes.

There are three major reasons why people get into tax trouble with the IRS and end up with a lien:

1. Employer failure to pay payroll taxes. Any time an employee gets a paycheck, the employer must withhold the employee's income tax, the employee's share of the social security, and Medicare obligation, and then send that money to the government. It's actually very common for a business to fall behind on sending that in.

2. Failure to pay ordinary income taxes.

3. Failure to pay a tax due on a forgiven debt. This kind of tax debt can come as a huge surprise.

If you negotiate a settlement on a debt (with a debt collector for example) and pay less than is due, the difference between what you actually owe and what you paid is counted as ordinary taxable income.

Say you owe $50,000 and your creditor agrees to accept $30,000 as payment in full. In that case the IRS considers the forgiven portion (the $20,000) to be taxable income. You're going to get a bill for the income tax on this amount.

So if any of the situations apply to you, you're going to receive a "Demand for Payment" and if you ignore it, it will allow the government to proceed to the next step in the collection process.

After you get the Demand for Payment, the government can then increase the pressure on you by filing a Notice of Federal Tax Lien (NFTL).

This formal legal document states the amount owed at the time the notice is filed, and it is usually filed in two places: (a) the registry of deeds in the county where you reside, and (b) the Secretary of State's office in the capital city of the state where you live.

Apart from telling the whole world about your tax troubles (very unpleasant), the filing of an NFTL has other serious consequences.

- It encumbers (ties up) any real estate or personal property that you own.

- It freezes (locks down) any bank accounts you have. Once an NFTL is filed in the county and state offices, your bank will soon know about it and your accounts can be frozen if you haven't agreed to a formal payment plan and kept it in good standing.

- It destroys your credit. If an NFTL is filed against you, it will soon find its way onto your credit report.

When a tax lien drops onto your credit report, it is going to be extremely difficult to get any new lines of credit.

Tax liens can remain on your credit report for at least 7 years. If you pay the amount or pay a negotiated settlement, your lien will be marked as satisfied. But what we ultimately want is a "withdrawal" (removal from the credit report).

Form 12277 (**https://www.irs.gov/pub/irs-pdf/f12277.pdf**) is how to formally ask the IRS

for a withdrawal. Your request must be in writing and provide the names and addresses of the credit reporting agencies, financial institutions and/or creditors that you want notified."

In layman's terms, it means you can ask the IRS to notify the credit reporting agencies (Equifax, Experian and TransUnion) that the lien has been withdrawn.

Even if you haven't paid the lien, a few years ago the IRS implemented something called the "Fresh Start" initiative, which is a series of procedures and policy changes directed toward taxpayers facing collections from the IRS. One of the changes includes a policy that allows

### Pro Tip: Good News!

Starting July 1, 2017, the three major credit agencies — Experian, Equifax and TransUnion — have stated that they are removing all tax liens and civil judgments from credit reports if they do not match three of the four criteria required: of name, address, social security number, and birthdate.

"It's good news for the consumer, clearly, because the credit score is used almost ubiquitously across the world of consumer finance, and lenders use it, insurance companies use it, credit carders use it," said John Ulzheimer, a credit consultant who has worked for Equifax and FICO, and resident CreditSecret.org specialist.

Ulzheimer also says the changes may not be permanent. "There is a possibility that if the credit reporting bureau is able to find the missing information, the negative information could reappear on consumer credit reports."

# Public Records

certain taxpayers to request that their tax liens be withdrawn, even before the underlying tax debt has been paid.

You may qualify for this, but there is no guarantee. To qualify for this program after the lien is released, you must usually meet the following 2 criteria:

1. You have been in compliance with the law for the past 3 years when it comes to filing individual, business, and information returns

2. You are current on all estimated tax payments and federal tax deposits

To qualify for the program while the lien is *still* being paid, you must generally meet the following 6 criteria:

1. You qualify as a taxpayer.

2. You owe no more than $25,000.

3. The Direct Debit Installment Agreement must be on track to pay off the entire amount within 60 months, or before the Collection Statute expires, whichever is earlier.

4. You are fully compliant with all other payment and filing requirements.

5. You have made at least 3 consecutive payments in the direct debit payment plan.

6. You have never defaulted on a Direct Debit Installment agreement.

If you meet either of these sets of criteria, you may be eligible to have the tax lien withdrawn from your credit report. If so, go on to the next steps.

1. After paying off your balance in full or being granted a waiver for your unpaid balance, you should receive IRS Form 668(Z), Release of Federal Tax Lien

2. Find your original IRS Form 668(Y), Notice of Federal Tax Lien

3. Fill out IRS Form 12277, Application for Withdrawal of Filed Form 668(Y)

4. Submit all 3 of the above documents to the IRS, along with an explanation of why you are requesting the lien to be withdrawn.

5. After some time for processing, you should receive IRS Form 10916(c), Withdrawal of Filed Notice of Federal Tax Lien.

6. You will use IRS Form 10916(c) and send it to the credit bureaus.

## For State Taxes:

After paying your tax lien in full, you will need to contact your state tax office and request a form verifying the release of the lien. This process will differ by state. If you have an unpaid state tax lien, you can use the method below for removing it from your credit reports (although legally you will still owe the debt).

# The Loophole to Remove Liens, Judgments And Bankruptcies (public records) From Your Credit Report

When a public record is filed against you, it is filed with a court. Whether or not you get it removed from your credit reports, that has no effect on having it removed from court records. So eventually, you should do your best to pay those and have them removed from court records. But in the short term, if you want a public record off of your credit report, here's what you could do...

When you look at your credit report, it shows who furnished the information. But if you look specifically at the public records section of your report, you will see that the bureaus claim the furnisher is the "recorder of deeds", "magistrate" or "municipal court". Sometimes it may just show the court address.

The problem is, none of that information is accurate. The recorder of deeds, the magistrate, or the court itself did not furnish any of this information to the credit bureaus.

Our members have obtained letters from courts over and over again, and they all confirm the same thing - that they do NOT furnish information to any third party, including the credit bureaus.

So why would the credit bureaus provide you with false information about who furnished the information?

We don't know the answer to that.

But what we do know is that the bureaus get public records information from companies like "Lexis-Nexis", or sometimes "PACER". Typically it is from Lexis Nexis, which is a "for profit" company that is in the information-selling business. They regularly collect public records information into their database, and then they sell it to the credit bureaus.

We have no idea why the credit bureaus do not list Lexis-Nexis as their information provider. Whatever the reason, it is your loophole to getting public records removed, because it is a violation of the Fair Credit Reporting Act to report false information.

And claiming to get information from a court, when it is actually obtained

**Michael W**
February 8 at 5:03pm

1st SMCWIN !!!!!! Trans Union has finally removed my paid federal tax lien off my credit report. I followed the advice of others I submitted the letter from the San Diego recorders office stating that they do not report to the credit agencies along with filing a IRS form 10916 (Withdrawal of Filed Notice of Federal Tax Lien),the IRS sent to Trans Union the recorded lien withdrawl certificates to both agencies Trans Union and Equifax. I'm filing a complaint with the CFPB against Equifax who is still playing hardball I did not file a complaint with the CFPB against them like I should have done it when I filed against Trans Union I'm currently in the process of doing it now.

# Liens, Judgments And Bankruptcies

from an unnamed 3rd party, could easily be considered "false information" on your credit report.

Furthermore, when you dispute a public record with the credit bureaus, they will sometimes go so far as to say they VERIFIED the information with the court! Again, this is completely false. They typically utilize an automated computerized system called e-Oscar (Online Solution for Complete and Accurate Reporting) that automatically checks with Lexis-Nexis. The dispute is broken down into a 2 or 3 digit code and sent to Lexis-Nexis for verification. (NOT to the court and NOT by a real live person)

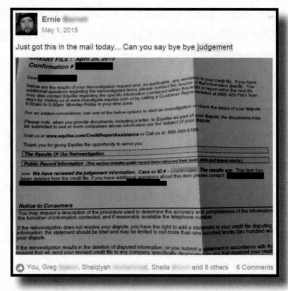

That is precisely why we provide you with letters that use words to get HUMAN attention, rather than automated, error prone systems.

By now you should be starting to see why you have a real opportunity to get all of your public records removed. It is clear that the bureaus are providing false information on your report when they claim to get the information directly from the courts.

You can actually go down to your courthouse and get one of these letters for yourself. Or you can send them a letter, asking for an answer in return. In fact, we recommend it.

## Pro Tip: Mix It Up!

Staples, different colored paper, different sized paper, and different fonts can confuse the automated system and force a real live person to review your letters.

First of all, it is sad and disgraceful that your heart felt letters, backed with proof, are reduced to a 2 digit code by a computer algorithm.

In order to create a paper trail, send a letter to the clerk of the court where the public record was filed. In the letter, request the procedure for verifying records with the credit reporting agencies. Enclose a self-addressed stamped envelope so that they can easily send you a reply.

Now you will have proof that the courts do not verify information directly with the credit reporting agencies.

They will provide you with a letter similar to this:

---

## United States Bankruptcy Court
### Western District of Virginia

Office of the Clerk
United States Courthouse and Federal Building, Room 223
116 North Main Street
Harrisonburg, Virginia 22802

John W. L. Craig, II
Clerk of Court

(540)434-8327
FAX (540)434-9715

November 4, 2016

Re:

Dear

We are in receipt of your letter dated October 24, 2016, requesting court's procedure for verifying information with the credit bureaus..

The U.S. Bankruptcy Court does not report to the credit bureaus, and therefore, we have no control over the information contained in your report. You may wish to work directly with your credit bureau or perhaps contact an attorney for assistance.

Sincerely,

Deputy Clerk

CreditReportLtrH.frm

---

All of the above is plenty of ammunition to show the credit bureaus the error in reporting, and to get your public records removed.

# Advanced Public Records Removal

To go even one step further in getting more ammunition for public records removal, some of our members have done the following:

## The Security "Freeze" Trick

We previously spoke about how the credit bureaus actually obtain public records data from LexisNexis, and not the public courts that they claim to.

As a consumer, and depending on the state of your residency, you may be able to request that a "security freeze" be placed on certain data that LexisNexis® Risk Solutions maintains about you, including some or all of the following: C.L.U.E. reports, Current Carrier reports, and Riskview reports. You may also subsequently release or lift a freeze at a later date.

Furthermore, LexisNexis has an option to "opt out" from letting anyone access additional data on your reports with them. Placing a security freeze is as easy as making a phone call or visiting their website.

LexisNexis – (888) 497-9172

https://personalreports.lexisnexis.com/pdfs/mt_freeze_request.pdf

However, in order to additionally "opt out" of other services they provide (where they sell your information) you will need to provide them with evidence that you've potentially been a victim of identity fraud.

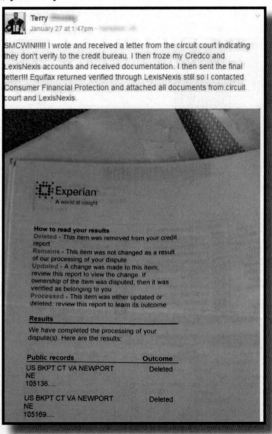

Terry ▬▬▬
January 27 at 1:47pm · ▬▬ ·

SMCWIN!!!!! I wrote and received a letter from the circuit court indicating they don't verify to the credit bureau. I then froze my Credco and LexisNexis accounts and received documentation. I then sent the final letter!!! Equifax returned verified through LexisNexis still so I contacted Consumer Financial Protection and attached all documents from circuit court and LexisNexis.

**Experian**
A world of insight

**How to read your results**
Deleted - This item was removed from your credit report
Remains - This item was not changed as a result of our processing of your dispute
Updated - A change was made to this item; review this report to view the change. If ownership of the item was disputed, then it was verified as belonging to you
Processed - This item was either updated or deleted; review this report to learn its outcome

**Results**
We have completed the processing of your dispute(s). Here are the results:

| Public records | Outcome |
|---|---|
| US BKPT CT VA NEWPORT NE 105136.... | Deleted |
| US BKPT CT VA NEWPORT NE 105169.... | Deleted |

Acceptable forms of proof are:

1. a police report

2. a copy of a letter from one of your creditors that identifies you as being a potential victim. Remember when there was a huge data breach at Target Department Stores? At that time millions of letters were mailed out to consumers indicating what happened, and stating that all affected customers were being provided with free credit monitoring for a short period of time in order to prevent any fraud. This type of thing happens often when banks are hacked. But now it will be good news for you because it gives you what you need to opt out of LexisNexis reporting altogether. If you've ever received one of these notices you can provide that to LexisNexis in order to "opt-out".

For more information on opting out, visit **http://www.lexisnexis.com/ privacy/for-consumers/opt-out-of-lexisnexis.aspx**

You may also want to freeze several of the other popular information brokers below, all who may be selling information about you.

Make sure to include the following necessary information:

1. First and last name
2. Social security number
3. Date of birth
4. Primary phone number
5. Address including ZIP code

Two of the following forms of identification:

1. A copy of a state-issued driver's license or state identification card.

2. A copy of a "recent" cable, utility, or phone statement with an address matching the address provided in Step 1. "Recent" is defined as no more than 60 days old from the date of IDA, Inc's receipt of a written request.

3. A copy of a SSN card.

4. A copy of a birth certificate.

5. A copy of a U.S. passport (picture page only).

6. A copy of a voided consumer check with an address matching the address you provided in Step 1.

7. A copy of an Alien Registration Card.

**CoreLogic Credco**
(877) 532-8778
**https://www.credco.com/ consumer/security-freeze.aspx**
CoreLogic Credco, LLC
Consumer Relations Department
Security Freeze Request
P.O. Box 509124
San Diego, CA 92150

**INNOVIS**
(800) 540-2505
**https://www.innovis.com/ personal/securityFreeze**
Innovis Consumer Assistance
PO Box 26
Pittsburgh, PA 15230-0026

**SageStream**
(888) 395-0277
**https://www.sagestreamllc.com/ security-freeze**
SageStream, LLC Consumer Office
P. O. Box 503793
San Diego, CA 92150
FAX (858) 312-6275

**ARS**
(800) 392-8911
(no website)
5005 Rockside Road, Suite 600
Independence, OH 44131 or fax:
216-615-7642

For additional companies and data brokers you may want to freeze, visit **http://www.stopdatamining.me**

In summary:

1. Obtain a letter from the court explaining that they do not provide information to the credit bureaus

2. Obtain a letter from Lexis Nexis verifying your security freeze and/or opt-opt.

3. Send Part 2 Letter # 1 to the credit bureau(s) reporting the public record (bankrupcty, tax lien or judgment)

4. If any of the bureaus reply and say they "verified" it, you can then open up a dispute with the CFPB (Consumer Financial Protection Bureau) and give them all of your evidence, including the letter from the court, as well as evidence of your security freeze/ optout.

After completing the above 4 steps you have a VERY good chance that the item(s) will be removed.

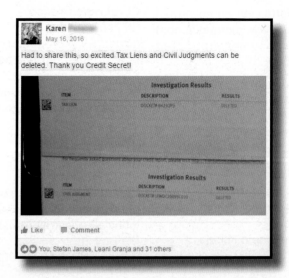

# CoreLogic and LexisNexis

We've talked a lot about LexisNexis, and also mentioned Credco. They are 2 additional credit bureaus that you can obtain reports from, and they sell your information to Equifax, Experian and TransUnion. Chances are, you will be amazed at how long they have been following you, and more importantly how much inaccurate information they have on you. So it is important to not only implement the "freeze" method mentioned earlier, but to clean up these reports as well.

They are both responsible for adhering to the laws of the FCRA just like the other credit bureaus. Don't let them try to fool you otherwise. In fact here is a link to a class-action settlement where LexisNexis allegedly attempted to skirt FCRA rules.

https://topclassactions.com/lawsuit-settlements/lawsuit-news/40030-lexisnexis-pays-13-5m-fair-credit-reporting-class-action-settlement

## Obtain Your Lexis-Nexis Report

To get a copy of the information that LexisNexis has in your consumer file with them, you will need to mail in a request.

First, you can download their form at: https://personalreports.lexisnexis.com.

Mail your form and verification documents to:

**LexisNexis**
Consumer Center
Attn: Full File Disclosure
P.O. Box 105108
Atlanta, GA 30348-5108

Once they have received your completed File Disclosure Request Form and verification documents, it will take them approximately 15 days to process your request.

## Disputing errors in your LexisNexis Report

Review your report for any derogatory information and use our template from Part 2, Letter 1 to dispute each item.

Send the letters to:

**LexisNexis Consumer Center**
P.O. Box 105108
Atlanta, GA, 30348

Upon receipt of your dispute, they have 30 days to conduct a reinvestigation of the information disputed and to record the current status of the information on your file or, in some instances, delete the information from your file.

Remember, they must adhere to the same rules as the other credit bureaus!

## Obtain Your CoreLogic Credco Consumer File

To obtain a copy of your CoreLogic Credco consumer file, you can call them at (877) 532-8778.

Or you can request a copy via mail sent to:

CoreLogic Credco, LLC
P.O. Box 509124
San Diego, CA 92150

## Disputing errors in your CoreLogic Credco Consumer File

Just like a credit report from the big three, Equifax, Experian, and TransUnion, CoreLogic Credco can contain errors. If you believe that something is wrong in your consumer file, then you can notify them just like you would the other credit bureaus, by starting with Part 2, Letter 1.

Their address is:

**CoreLogic Credco, LLC**
Consumer Relations Department
Consumer Disputes
P.O. Box 509124
San Diego, CA 92150

Once they receive this information, they will reinvestigate the disputed information, update your consumer file if their investigation determines that the information is incorrect, and send you the results, usually within 30 days.

Crystal ████████ ▓▓ celebrating success.
October 19, 2016

Took me 5 mths but I FINALY WON AGAINST MIDLAND FUNDING!!!!!!!!
Thank you CFPB
"The 3 major credit reporting agencies were notified to remove the collection tradeline. Midland takes consumer complaints serious and apologizes for the inconvenience caused to you"

👍 Like      💬 Comment

😊😊😊 You and 69 others

Tammy ████ ███████
November 24 · ███████

I am so thankful to have found this program. I started this around the first of August of this year, sent out all the first letters and had a credit score ranging from 500 - 550. I had a couple credit cards but didn't have a high credit limit on them. I used the shopping cart trick and was approved for a credit card for the following:

Victoria Secret
Brylane Home
New York & Co

Shortly after sending out the first letters, I left for a 2 month vacation. I checked my scores when I returned home, most everything has been removed from my credit reports or marked disputed, scores raised to mid 600s. I used the shopping cart trick again and was approved for a credit card for the following:

Buckle
Ann Taylor

Was also approved a business credit card from Capital One for my home based business. Also I was approved for a Kohls Crédit Card.

But the best thing is this Monday, I fullfilled a lifelong dream, was able to walk into my favorite Harley dealership, get financed by Harley Davidson financing on my own with no cosigner and rode this beautiful baby home. What a nice upgrade from my sportster.

So yes, this program does work. While I continue to work on my credit I'm also gonna start this program on my husbands credit reports.

Happy Thanksgiving everyone!

👍 Like      💬 Comment

😊😊😊 You, Stefan James, Brian ███ ██████ and 159 others

# Consumer Financial Protection Bureau (CFPB)

Launched in July 2011 as a supervisory and regulatory agency of the United States government, the CPFB is responsible for protecting the consumer in the financial sector. Technically, it protects every American and non-American using or relying on financial products and services. This is a good thing.

To many of us, the CFPB is still much of an unknown entity. Many questions still fly about as to what they do, where they derive their power, and who controls the watchmen. If we can draw precedence from history, the CFPB will, in the long run, be a best friend to the financial sector and a loyal friend to consumers alike. Hopefully, they will help us out with our credit reports along the way.

The empowerment of the CFPB marks the first time a federal regulatory agency has supervisory powers over credit bureaus. Interestingly, the bureau's hammer is not meant for just the big credit reporting agencies - Equifax, TransUnion, and Experian; the small ones are also subjected to their supervision. Around 30 companies, making up 94% of the industry are currently affected.

Everyone matters right now; both lesser known and influential. This is great news for us.

According to the CFPB website, "they are the government agencies charged with ensuring that banks, lenders and financial institutions treat consumers fairly." In its simplest form, the CFPB is empowered to make rules guiding how credit agencies operate. The Fair Credit Reporting Act (FCRA) says that the credit reporting agencies are required to do a "reinvestigation" if the accuracy of credit report data is in dispute. But the Act did not spell out the modalities for the reinvestigation,

# Filing a Complaint with the CFPB

If you have sent out the sequence of letters as outlined in this book, and had a few accounts that seem to be "stubborn" to remove, and you are reluctant to file a small claims suit, there is another option that many of our members are finding success with. A CFPB complaint only takes a few minutes to submit, and many members have seen accounts removed in two weeks or less.

Once you go to their website: **http://www.consumerfinance.gov/complaint** you can look through other consumer's complaints to get ideas of verbiage to use for your own complaint.

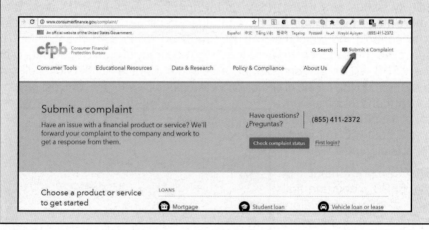

which is where the CFPB will come in.

Since the CFPB launched, consumers have benefited in numerous ways:

The CFPB successfully went after Discover, American Express, and Capital One, recovering around $400 million dollars for consumers. They also made the credit card companies pay fines and agree to stop offering add-on services to customers.

The CFPB ordered TransUnion and Equifax to pay over $23 million in fines and restitution for deceiving consumers about the usefulness of credit scores.

The CFPB went after Encore Capital Group (aka Midland Funding) and Portfolio Recovery Associates for alleged violations of the Fair Debt Collection Practices Act and received a $79 million dollar settlement.

# State Attorney General Complaints

Another option, for some rare cases, is to file a complaint with your State's Attorney General. The state attorney general in each of the 50 U.S. states and territories is the chief legal advisor to the state government and the state's chief law enforcement officer.

Before you begin, you should understand that not every complaint received by the Attorney General's office is going to have action taken on it. Your complaint can be used for the basis of an investigation or legal action against the company you are complaining about.

You can find out who your State Attorney General is, and how to contact them at: **http://www.naag.org/naag/attorneys-general/whos-my-ag.php**

# #SMCWIN !!

# The Better Business Bureau

If you get stuck dealing with a creditor, and you aren't ready to take them to small claims court yet, some members have had success reporting the companies to the BBB.

## What is the BBB?

The Better Business Bureau (BBB) is a group of private BBB organizations that promote a fair marketplace for both businesses and consumers. The organization gathers information regarding reliability, fraud, and ethical business practices and informs the public of scams and other business-related issues.

Whether or not the creditor/collector you are dealing with is accredited with the BBB, you can still file a complaint with your local BBB.

## Complaint Facts

The general turn around time for the BBB to close a complaint, is about 30 days, although it can be less. If a company chooses to not respond to the complaint, it will be reflected in their BBB Business Review and impact their BBB rating.

Keep in mind, the BBB has no legal power to force anyone to comply with its complaint resolution process. The only reason a company responds to a Better Business Bureau is to maintain a good reliability report.

Once the BBB reviews the complaint, and deems it within their guidelines, they will forward it to the creditor/collector within one to five business days. The creditor will have a set

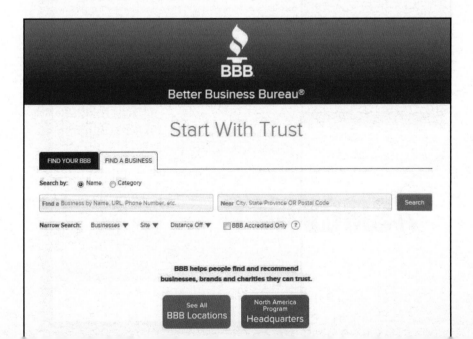

amount of time to respond. The BBB will notify you of the response and you'll have another 10 days to make a rebuttal, or the case will then be closed.

## How to File a Complaint

You can file a complaint over the phone or in writing, but the recommended way is to use the online complaint system.

Gather up all your supporting documentation, including the letters you've sent and any responses from the creditor.

Document what the issue is, in writing, outlining how you've tried to remedy the situation.

Be sure to clearly spell out the resolution you want. For example: "RESOLUTION HERE"

Once you have all of that ready to go, you can file your complaint by visiting www.bbb.org. From that home page, select "Contact" at the bottom of the screen.

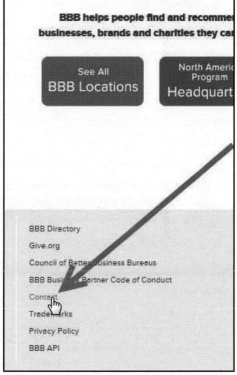

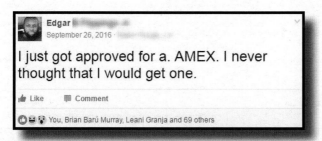

# The Better Business Bureau

On the new screen, select the link to "I want to file a complaint."

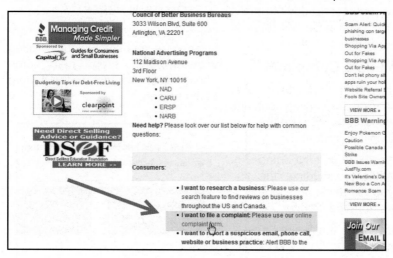

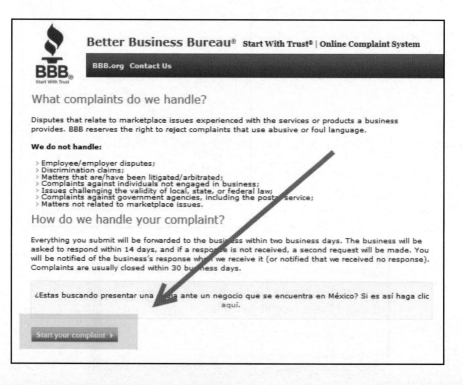

The first screen of the complaint form asks you to verify the nature of your complaint.

You will need to select the following option:

Business product or service

Answer the military service question and choose Next.

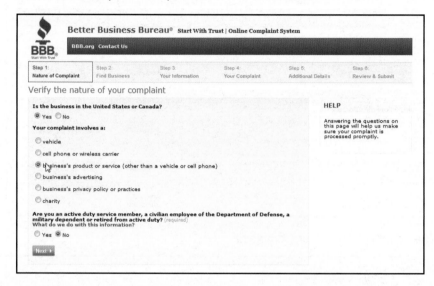

Now you have to search for the company to make the complaint about. For this example we used Portfolio Recovery Collection Agency.

The online complaint form has a search feature that lets you search for the company by using its full name or part of the name. You can also search by location, using the name of the city, state or zip code.

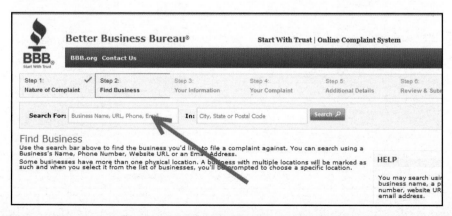

# The Better Business Bureau

You are required to identify the specific location for the business. If you cannot provide this information, you will have to find it or you will not be able to proceed with the online complaint form.

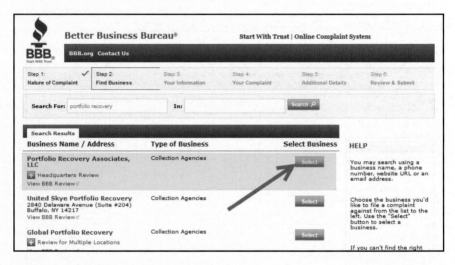

Then choose: Start Your Complaint.

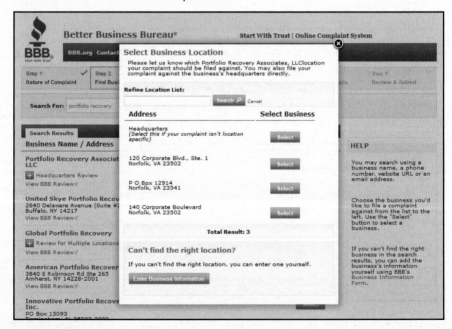

After you identify business and its location, you may be redirected to another screen. Your complaint will then be handled by the local or regional branch of the BBB where the business is located. You will need to proceed by answering the questions that are presented.

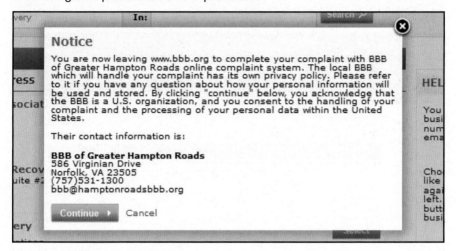

You will be asked a few questions about your complaint, and receive some terms and conditions before you can move on. Answer and press Submit.

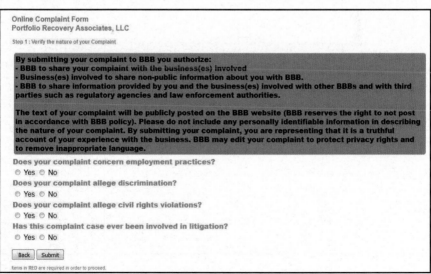

# The Better Business Bureau

Now you have to complete the next section of the online complaint form by providing your name, address, telephone number, and other contact information. If you leave any of the required information blank, you will not be allowed to proceed with filing your complaint.

Step 3 of the process will ask you to confirm the location of the business you are filing the complaint about.

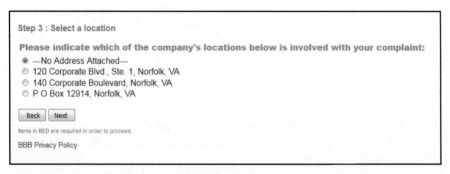

In Step 4, you will choose the category your complaint falls under. For this example we chose "Billing or Collection Issues".

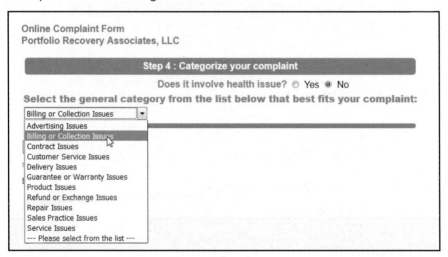

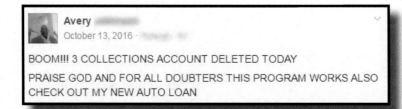

# The Better Business Bureau

The next section of the online complaint form provides you with a blank text areas to explain your complaint. You may write as much as necessary (up to the form limits posted) to explain your complaint. When completing this section of the online complaint form, remember that the text of your complaint will be posted on BBB websites. Therefore, you should not include any personally identifying information in the text that you write. Do not include names, telephone numbers or account numbers.

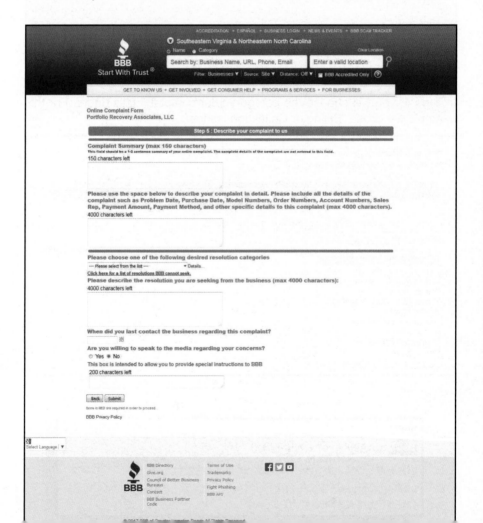

Remain professional and keep it brief. Provide only the relevant details. You do not need to repeat every single part of the transaction or any subsequent conversations. Focus on the relevant details of your dispute.

You will have to choose your desired resolution category.

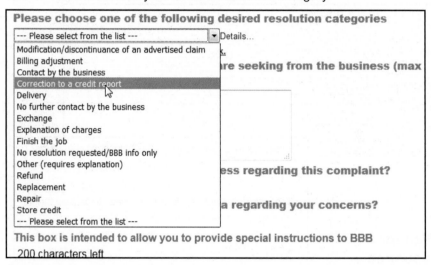

When you are finished with filling out your complaint, press Submit. You will be redirected to a screen that contains all the information you have just submitted.

# The Better Business Bureau

You can click the link at the bottom of this screen that says "View the status of your complaint" in order to upload or add any additional information to the complaint.

**BBB CASE#: 48063561**

*** If you have information you would like to provide regarding this complaint or need to upload a document, click **her**

| | |
|---|---|
| Complaint filed by: | Tom Doe **(More)** |
| Complaint filed against: | Portfolio Recovery Associates, LLC **(More)** |
| Complaint status: | Case Received by BBB **(More)** |
| Case Description: | Nam consectetur lorem non felis venenatis lacinia. Vestibulum ante ipsum primis in faucibus orci luctus et ultrices posuere cubilia Curae;... **(More)** |
| BBB Designated Category: | Billing or Collection Issues |
| Case opened date: | 02/02/2017 |
| Case closed date: | |
| Desired Resolution: | Lorem ipsum dolor sit amet, consectetur adipiscing elit. Pellentesque congue velit tellus, ut dapibus mauris dapibus sed. Nulla suscipit... **(More)** |

**Optional: You may download a copy of**
Once you have submitted your response, yo
reponse by clicking the link above.

**Please make your comments below (max 9000 characters)**

9000 characters left

**To submit files with this information, click the Browse button**

Browse... No file selected.

Back    Submit

## Wait for a response

The BBB will process your complaint as soon as you submit it. Within two business days, they will forward your complaint to the business that you have identified. The business will be expected to reply with fourteen days. If the BBB does not receive a reply within that time, they will make a second request.

When the company responds to the BBB, you will then receive a copy of that response. If the company does not respond, then the BBB will send you a notice that no response was received. If the BBB does not receive a response within 30 days after the filing of your complaint, the complaint will be closed.

If the company submits a response, you will receive a copy of it. The company may agree with your complaint and consent to your requested remedy. Alternatively, the company may stand on its earlier decision.

Summary:

Combining the power of the CFPB, the Attorney General's Office, and the BBB can put pressure on a collection agency, a creditor, or a credit bureau to do the right thing!

# Other Types of Letters

## What To Do When A Deleted Credit Item Is Re-Inserted

Congratulations! You've managed to remove negative items from your credit report! Your work is not done though. You must continually monitor your credit reports in case the company gets sneaky and re-inserts a negative item.

When you challenged your derogatory/unsubstantiated/inaccurate items, the creditors and/or credit bureaus had 30 days to complete their investigation pursuant to your dispute. If the item cannot be verified within 30 days then they would remove it because they are not allowed to maintain information that is unverifiable. However, if the item is verified on day 31 or any day afterwards, the creditors can re-report, and the credit bureau can reinsert the item in your credit reports.

If a previously removed item is reinserted, the Fair Credit Reporting Act (FCRA) requires the credit reporting agency to notify you no later than five business days after the date of reinsertion. This FCRA requirement is rarely followed. Additionally, the creditor who reinserts the negative item must also certify the information is correct.

Here is the exact law pertaining to this situation:

## 15 U.S. Code § 1681i - FCRA 611 (a)(5)(B)(ii)

*Notice to consumer:*

*If any information that has been deleted from a consumer's file pursuant to subparagraph (A) is reinserted in the file, the consumer reporting agency shall notify the consumer of the reinsertion in writing not later than 5 business days after the reinsertion or, if authorized by the consumer for that purpose, by any other means available to the agency.*

If you find a previously deleted item has been re-inserted without written notification, you could send the following letter:

# 5 Day Reinsertion Letter

Send to the credit bureau if an item is removed and later placed back on your credit report.

Your Name
Your Address
Credit Bureau Name
Credit Bureau Address
Date

RE: Social Security Number: 000-00-0000

To Whom It May Concern,

On [insert date of original letter] I disputed an account reported by [insert name of collection agency, creditor or court] in the file you maintain under my Social Security number.

I was informed on [insert date of deletion] that the item was deleted from my credit report.

Now I have discovered that the item has been reinserted on my credit report.

In accordance with the requirements of the FCRA section 611(a)(5)(B) (ii), you are required to notify me of the reinsertion in writing within 5 business days.

*(B)Requirements relating to reinsertion of previously deleted material*

*(ii)Notice to consumer*

*If any information that has been deleted from a consumer's file pursuant to subparagraph (A) is reinserted in the file, the consumer reporting agency shall notify the consumer of the reinsertion in writing not later than 5 business days after the reinsertion or, if authorized by the consumer for that purpose, by any other means available to the agency.*

I received no such notification. This is a very serious violation of the FCRA, and I reserve the right to pursue legal action for your blatant disregard for the law.

I hereby demand that you immediately delete the item from my credit report in order to avoid legal action. I am submitting this complaint separately to the Consumer Financial Protection Bureau, the Attorney General's Office, and the BBB.

Please govern yourself accordingly.

Your Name (typed not signed)
Your SSN
Your Address

Cc: Consumer Financial Protection Bureau
Cc: Attorney General's Office
Cc: Better Business Bureau

You can also initiate a complaint with the Consumer Financial Protection Bureau. The complaint would be against the credit bureau. They will not ignore an inquiry from the CFPB.

Alternatively, you could also file a small claims lawsuit against the credit bureau for re-inserting the item without notice, in violation of the Fair Reporting Credit Act (FCRA) § 611 (15 U.S.C. § 1681I)(a)(5)(B)(ii).

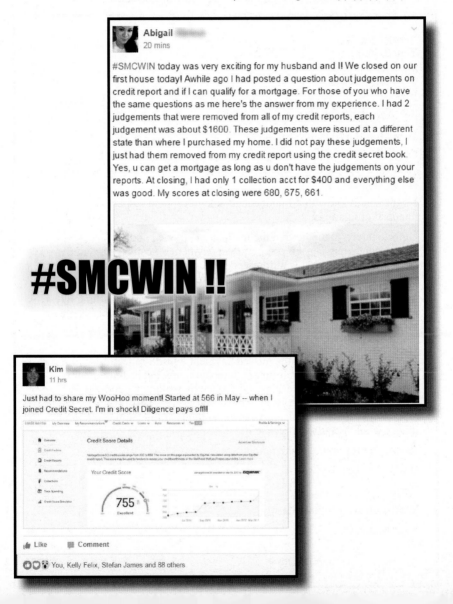

**Abigail**
20 mins

#SMCWIN today was very exciting for my husband and I! We closed on our first house today! Awhile ago I had posted a question about judgements on credit report and if I can qualify for a mortgage. For those of you who have the same questions as me here's the answer from my experience. I had 2 judgements that were removed from all of my credit reports, each judgement was about $1600. These judgements were issued at a different state than where I purchased my home. I did not pay these judgements, I just had them removed from my credit report using the credit secret book. Yes, u can get a mortgage as long as u don't have the judgements on your reports. At closing, I had only 1 collection acct for $400 and everything else was good. My scores at closing were 680, 675, 661.

**#SMCWIN !!**

**Kim**
11 hrs

Just had to share my WooHoo moment! Started at 566 in May -- when I joined Credit Secret. I'm in shock! Diligence pays off!!

Credit Score Details

Your Credit Score

**755**
Excellent

👍 Like    💬 Comment

You, Kelly Felix, Stefan James and 88 others

# Goodwill Letter

Sometimes you may have an open account with a creditor that is mostly on favorable terms. In that case you may not want to ruffle their feathers too much. But perhaps you have 1 or 2 late pays on the account that are hurting you.

For that scenario we recommend a goodwill letter where you politely ask for forgiveness.

---

Your Name
Your Address
Creditor Name
Creditor Address
Date

RE: Account # (insert account number)

To Whom It May Concern,

I'm writing to you because I noticed that my most recent credit report contains a late payment reported on [insert date(s)] for my [insert company name] account.

I want you to know that I understand, and have great respect for my financial obligations.

Unfortunately, at the time of the incident mentioned above, I had [insert circumstance that caused you to miss a payment – hospital stay/injury/job loss/etc]. Aside from this unforeseen and unavoidable circumstance, you will see that I have an excellent payment record.

In the near future, I am planning on applying for [insert something like a mortgage/auto loan/loan for my daughter's wedding], and it has come to my attention that the missed payment on my credit reports could hurt my ability to qualify.

In my heart, I know that the missed payment doesn't reflect my creditworthiness and commitment to repaying my debts. I am humbly asking for you to give me a second chance by making a goodwill adjustment to remove the late payment on [insert date(s)] from my credit reports. As I understand it, you can do so in just a few minutes of your time. I would greatly appreciate it!

Thank you for your consideration.

Have a blessed day!

Best,

Your Name (typed not signed)
Your Address

---

# Incomplete/Missing Info Letter

If you acknowledge that a negative item is definitely yours, you can always opt to challenge it in a different way, instead of just saying "not mine". If that's the case, you can send a version of the letter below to get it removed on a technicality, such as missing or incomplete information. One of our favorites is challenging an item based on an incorrect account number, as some credit bureaus report an account number something like this: Acct # 12345XXXXX

It is said that they may be doing this for your privacy protection, but the FTC opinion letter here says quite the opposite: **https://www.ftc.gov/policy/advisory-opinions/advisory-opinion-darcy-06-30-00**

*"In sum, it is our view that a CRA that always scrambles or truncates account (or social security) numbers does not technically comply with Section 609 because it does not provide "accurate" (and perhaps not "clear") disclosure of "all information" in the file."*

They basically state that by not reporting the entire account number, they are not reporting 100% accurate information as required by section 609 of the Fair Credit Reporting Act.

---

Your Name
Your Address
Credit Bureau Name
Credit Bureau Address
Date

Send to the credit bureau to remove incomplete items (for example an incorrect acct #, balance, incorrect or missing status)

RE: Social Security Number: 000-00-0000

To Whom It May Concern,

I am writing to challenge the reporting and compliance on an account with [insert company name] that is being reported on my credit report with incorrect/missing info.

More specifically, I am referencing the fact that you are reporting

[insert condition such as "an incorrect high balance", "an incorrect account number", "an undated late pay", "a missing field of [insert missing field here such as status]", "the wrong account type", "an incorrect credit limit", "a late pay after account was closed", "an inaccurate date of last activity", "an inaccurate date of last update", "a charge off listed as "open", "a collection account with a limit", "an inaccurate reporting date"].

Your improper procedures are highly damaging to my credit score. Please immediately delete this item.

Your Name (printed or typed, not signed)
SSN
Address

Cc: Consumer Financial Protection Bureau
Cc: Attorney General's Office
Cc: Better Business Bureau

# Returned Mail Letter

Sometimes you may mail a letter to a creditor or collection agency, using the address shown on your credit report. If that mail comes back returned as undeliverable, you may have grounds for removal. After all, the credit bureau is not allowed to report anything they know to be false, including addresses. In that case you could send the following letter.

Send to the credit bureau to dispute an item that came back as returned mail when you contacted the creditor or collection agency.

---

Your Name
Your Address
Credit Bureau Name
Credit Bureau Address
Date

RE: Social Security Number: 000-00-0000

To Whom It May Concern,

There is currently an inaccurate item being reported on my credit report from [insert company name]. I have contacted this company at the address listed on my credit report here:

[insert address here]

As you can see, I have enclosed a photocopy of my mail being returned from the post office due to an invalid address.

Given that the furnisher has provided false information to you about me, and provided you with a false address, I demand that the item they are reporting be removed immediately.

Your Name (printed or typed, not signed)
SSN
Address

Cc: Consumer Financial Protection Bureau
Cc: Attorney General's Office
Cc: Better Business Bureau

---

## Alternative/Bizarre Letter

This final letter is a bizarre letter that just works many times. We have no reason to explain it other than it was provided to us by a mathematician who wishes to remain anonymous. He has sent over 45,000 dispute letters to the credit bureaus and noted which keywords and phrases resulted in the most removals. We have verified that this letter does indeed work very often.

Can be used for most circumstances, sent to the credit bureau – note that

# Alternative/Bizarre Letter

the misspellings and grammar errors are on purpose – this letter is highly effective at making the bureau's automated systems not comprehend, therefore requiring a real employee to review (and hopefully remove) it.

---

Your Name
Your Address
Credit Bureau Name
Credit Bureau Address
Date

RE: Social Security Number: 000-00-0000 and account reported from [insert company name] with account # [insert account #]

ALL REPORTED DATA MUST BE COMPLETE,CORRECT,AND PROVEN IF CHALLENGED.I DO NOT GRANT YOU AUTHORITY TO REPORT VERSUS ME WITHOUT ADEQUATE COMLIANCE OF STATE AND FEDERAL LAWS BEING APPLICABLE THROUGHOUT. AS SUCH I DEMAND DELETION IMMEDIATELY OF YOUR DECLARED CLAIMS AGAINST ME.PER COMMON LAW,YOU ARE DEMANDED TO DEMONSTRATE THAT YOU CAN AND HAVE WILLINGNESS TO ABSOLUTELY VERIFY AND VALIDATE (OR JUST SAY "CERTIFICATE") EVERY AND ONE EVEN EACH ANY AND OR ALL ALLEGATIONS YET PHYSICALLY DEFICIENT OR UNPROVEN MINE, CHALLENGED OR NOT.NOTE THE UNLAWFULNESS AND VILE INFRINGEMENT CREATED POTENTIALLY VERSUS ME SHOULD YOU CONTINUE TO RETAIN REPORT  RESTRUCTURE RESELL RETURN OR ELSE WISE EVERY AND ONE EVEN EACH ANY OR ALL DATA ,NOTATIONS ,DATES, BALANCES ,CALCULATIONS, AUDITS, ACCOUNTING RECORDS,REQUISITE 426-CHARACTER FORMAT FIELDED P6 STATEMENT(S), MANDATED 386 PARCELS OF CONFIRMATION NECCESSARY TO REPORT A COLLECTION ACTIVITY AND OR DEBT ALLEGED, THE MINIMAL FIVE (5) PORTIONED PERSONAL IDENTIFIERS, THE ALPHA-/ NUMERIC-/AND OR ALPHANUMERIC SOURCE CODE(S),AS WELL AS EVERY AND ONE EVEN ANY OR ALL LEGISTRATIONS,ACTS,ARTICLES,PARAGRAPHS,-STATEMENTS,REGULATIONS, OBLIGATIONS OR OTHERWISE REQUIRED,WHETHER MENTIONED OR NOT.ANNUL IN BRIEF TODAY EVEN RIGHT NOW   AND DO SO THEREAFTER MINUS ANY RESULTANT PREJUDICES AND OR INJURIES TO ME, REAL OR IMAGINED, WITHAL.

Your Name (printed or typed, not signed)

# Chapter 4: Lawsuits

None of this is legal advice! Always seek out a lawyer if you are looking for legal advice. (preferably one who specializes in FCRA or FDCPA law)

Alternatively check out LegalShield for low cost legal advice: **http://creditsecret.org/legalshield**

## Small Claims Court

If the credit bureaus, creditors or collection agencies are not following the law, not responding, not providing legitimate proof, within the required timeframes, harassing you, etc, and you are fed up with sending letters, you can opt to file a small claims lawsuit.

Keep in mind that most of the people reading this will never need to resort to this.

But some members have found success with going down to their local courthouse and filing a "Small Claims Lawsuit". It typically costs very little to file a small claims suit, and it only takes a few minutes.

The cost to file depends on how much you are suing for. FCRA rules allow for up to $1,000 per violation.

However, it has always been our belief that the amount is irrelevant because the goal is not to win money - the goal is to win removal of the negative/unverifiable/inaccurate item.

So you could always sue for a small amount, because even if you win $100, you will likely win removal as well. And if not, you can use the judgment as leverage to get removal.

Now the important thing is to not get nervous. You will not likely have to go to court. Most cases are settled well before the trial date, or through court mandated mediation, where a court appointed mediator will try to get both sides to come to an amicable resolution.

If you do find yourself required to appear, due to not settling prior, we recommend visiting your local courthouse to watch how other cases are handled. That way you will be familiar with the procedures.

One other advantage of small claims action is that the creditor/collection agency or credit bureau is required to come to you. Meaning they will need to fly out to your location to defend themselves. That could be a great expense for them. Given that small claims actions are not allowed to cover attorney fees, if they send a legal team, even if they win the case, you would not be liable to pay their attorney fees.

To find the small claims court nearest you, simply do a Google search for "small claims court" in your city or state and follow the directions, as each state is different. Sometimes they charge you a higher filing fee, depending on how much you are suing for. So you may want to just do the minimum, since the goal is not to win any money, it's to get your derogatory/unfair/inaccurate items removed.

# Examples of What You Could Potentially File Suit For and Against Whom

| Who | Reason | Law | Fine |
|-----|--------|-----|------|
| Creditors, if they report your credit history inaccurately. | Defamation, financial injury | US Court of Appeals, Ninth Circuit, No. 00-15946, Nelson vs. Chase Manhattan | Extent of damages incurred by the wronged party as deemed by the courts. |
| Creditors, if you dispute a debt, and they fail to report it as disputed to the credit bureaus. | Protection under the FCRA | FCRA Section 623 | $1,000 |
| Creditors, if they pull your credit file without permissible purpose. | Injury to your credit report and credit score | FCRA Section 604(A)(3) | $1,000 |
| Credit bureaus, if they refuse to correct information after being provided proof of inaccuracy. | Defamation, willful injury | FCRA Section 623<br><br>CUSHMAN, v. TRANS UNION CORPORATION US Court of Appeals for the Third Circuit Court Case 115 F.3d 220<br><br>June 9, 1997, Filed (D.C. No. 95-cv-01743). | Extent of damages incurred by the wronged party, as deemed by the courts. |
| Credit bureaus, if they reinsert a deleted item from your credit report without notifying you in writing within 5 business days. | Consumer protection afforded by the FCRA | FCRA Part (A)(5)(B)(ii) | $1,000 |
| Credit bureaus, if they fail to respond to your written disputes within 30 days (a 15 day extension may be granted if they receive information from the creditor within the first 30 days). | Consumer protection afforded by the FCRA | FCRA Section 611 Part (A)(1) | $1,000 |

# Examples Continued

| Who | Reason | Law | Fine |
|---|---|---|---|
| Creditors, collection agencies, or credit bureaus, if they "Re-Age" your account by reporting the date of last activity instead of the date of first delinquency. | Consumer protection afforded by the FCRA | FCRA Section 605(c) | $1,000 |
| Collection agency, if they fail to report a disputed debt to the credit bureaus. | Protection under the FDCPA | FDCPA Section 807(8) | $1,000 |
| Collection Agency, if they do not validate your debt yet continue to pursue collection activity by filing for a judgment. | Consumer protection afforded by the FDCPA | FDCPA Section 809(b), FTC opinion letter Cass from LeFevre . | $1,000 |
| Collection Agency, if you have sent them a cease and desist letter and they still call you. | Consumer protection afforded by the FDCPA | FDCPA Section 805(c) | $1,000 |
| Collection Agency, if they have not validated your debt and they still continue to report to the credit bureaus. | Consumer protection afforded by the FDCPA | FDCPA Section 809(b) FTC opinion letter Cass from LeFevre | $1,000 |
| Collection Agency, if they call you after 9 PM at night or before 8 AM. | Consumer protection afforded by the FDCPA | FDCPA Section 805(a)(1) | $1,000 |
| Collection Agency, if they call you at work when you have advised them that you do not want these calls. | Consumer protection afforded by the FDCPA | FDCPA Section 805(a)(3) | $1,000 |

## Examples Continued

| Who | Reason | Law | Fine |
|---|---|---|---|
| Collection Agency, if they call any third party about your debt such as friends, neighbors, relatives. | Consumer protection afforded by the FDCPA | FDCPA Section 805(b) | $1,000 |
| Collection agency, if they use any kind of harassment or abuse. | Consumer protection afforded by the FDCPA | FDCPA Section 806 | $1,000 |
| Collector cannot claim to seize property or have you arrested. | Consumer protection afforded by the FDCPA | FDCPA Section 807 | $1,000 |
| Collector must be in the county in which you lived when you signed the original contract for the debt or where you live at the time when they file the lawsuit. | Consumer protection afforded by the FDCPA | FDCPA Section 811(a)(2) | $1,000 |

**Esperanza**
Yesterday at 10:52am

Ladies and gentlemen let me just say this program is awesome 👍. I started this program about a year and a half ago with my scores in the 400's now I have removed all negative information from all 3 credit reports. And now my scores are 700 and above. Within the last month or so I have increased limits on all my old credit cards and applied for new ones. Chase card $4500, American Express $ 2000, Capital One $1000, Best Buy Visa $ 3000, Barcade with Apple Rewards $2000, Dillard's American Express $3600 and a host of other retail cards. And yesterday I signed up with Pen Fed for a 15,000 loan and another $1000 credit ▇. This program will allow you to reach goals like never before. Just follow the book. #SMCWIN

# Tips During Court

Bring a 3 ring binder of proof - all examples of where you believe the defendant violated your rights. Use a highlighter on the main points. This may include letters you sent, their replies, copies of your credit reports, and anything dated like a certified mail receipt.

Print out and highlight the sections of the FCRA or FDCPA that you believe they violated.

The judge may ask to review your evidence, and may even keep your binder for a few days to arrive at a decision later once they have brushed up on the specific laws you are claiming - make it easy for them!

Include a summary of bullet points that you can refer to, with the top points you'd like to get across.

Do NOT get emotional or waste anyone's time. Simply state the facts.

If the other side doesn't show up, the judge may still ask to hear your evidence. If they do, make sure that you ask for a default judgment! Some judges won't issue it unless you ask for it.

If you can prove damages, you will typically be in a better position. Examples of damages may be: denial of credit, being forced to pay higher interest rates, etc. Also, as in many example cases you will find later in this chapter, mental anguish and humiliation can be considered as actual damages.

Here are some examples of things that could conceivably happen in a small claims courtroom:

## Example Scenarios

**Defendant:** "Your honor, here is a bill (or other document) that shows the plaintiff did not pay X amount."

**Answer:** "Objection: no foundation" - this means you haven't established the authenticity or accuracy of a piece of evidence.

**Defendant:** "Your honor, mr./mrs. X opened an account with X company on X date."

**Answer:** "Objection" - "Was the defendant/attorney personally present when the alleged account was opened on X date? How does he/she have firsthand knowledge? If they weren't there then this is hearsay."

**Defendant:** presents the court with a document and says "Is this your signature?"

**Answer:** "Let the record show I am looking at what appears to be an 8.5 by 11 inch piece of white paper with what appears to be some sort of photocopy on it. Based on the way you asked the question, and if I understand you correctly, I would have to say no - I have never seen this piece of paper or photocopy before, so I cannot determine with absolute certainty whether or not the document is authentic or if that is my signature."

## Mediation

Some states require or recommend mediation prior to actually hearing a case - keep in mind that the mediator may know the defendant's attorney personally, and it may not be in your best interests to give up if they tell you that you "don't have a case". Giving up during or after mediation is completely up to you, but it is a guaranteed loss rather than learning from the meeting and being better prepared for the actual court date.

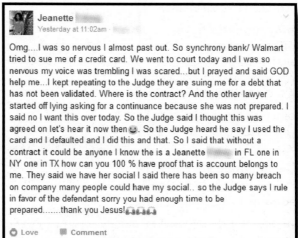

Jeanette
Yesterday at 11:02am

Omg....I was so nervous I almost past out. So synchrony bank/ Walmart tried to sue me of a credit card. We went to court today and I was so nervous my voice was trembling I was scared...but I prayed and said GOD help me...I kept repeating to the Judge they are suing me for a debt that has not been validated. Where is the contract? And the other lawyer started off lying asking for a continuance because she was not prepared. I said no I want this over today. So the Judge said I thought this was agreed on let's hear it now then 😊. So the Judge heard he say I used the card and I defaulted and I did this and that. So I said that without a contract it could be anyone I know the is a Jeanette [ ] in FL one in NY one in TX how can you 100 % have proof that is account belongs to me. They said we have her social I said there has been so many breach on company many people could have my social.. so the Judge says I rule in favor of the defendant sorry you had enough time to be prepared.......thank you Jesus!

Love    Comment

You, Steve Solem, Kelly Felix and 515 others

## What to do if YOU Are Sued

Whether you have been served with a lawsuit or you will in the future, the most important thing to remember is - ANSWER IT.

Some debt collectors are notorious for filing dozens of cases every day against people they want to collect from, knowing that most won't show up. A no-show can turn into a default judgment, and a judgment can turn into wage garnishment and all sorts of issues.

Here is a great article from a law firm in New Jersey about the DO's and DON'Ts of getting sued, especially

## Member Stories

Here is what one of our successful members mentioned about his own court date when he was sued:

M[ ] I got sued before and I went to court and my defense was I've had lots of credit cards so I'm not sure if thats mine . Can they provide my signature as proof that that account is mine. They showed all kinds of ols bills and statements and asked if I recognized them . I said I can't be sure.since I've had lots of credit cards. Can they provide a signature to prove thats mine. They didn't have the signature so the case was dismissed.

Unlike · Reply · 9 · 20 hrs

as it relates to collections:

http://yournjattorneys.
com/pressler-and-
pressler-lawsuit-dos-and-
donts (we are not affiliated
with this company)

Another great article about
being sued can be found
here:

https://toughnickel.com/
personal-finance/You-Can-Beat-
Credit-Card-Debt-Collectors

Here are a few interesting stories
regarding big collection agencies
such as Midland Funding and
Portfolio Associates:

http://www.dailykos.com/
story/2010/4/5/854290 - woman
sues debt collector and wins $8.1
million

http://blog.credit.com/2015/09/2-
of-americas-largest-debt-
collectors-will-refund-60-million-
to-consumers-125132 - federal
regulators force 2 debt collectors to
refund $60 million

And here are some cases you may
want to review using Google (some
of these might be helpful to have in
your binder if you go to court) - you
can always Google "FCRA cases" or
FDCPA cases" to get an expanded
list of recent important cases as well.

## Liability

**Spears/Brennan Appeal from the
Marion Superior Court** - The judge
ruled the following: "As discussed
previously, an FDCPA claim has
nothing to do with whether the
underlying debt is valid. An FDCPA
claim concerns the method of
collecting the debt. It does not arise
out of the transaction creating the
debt [.] Azar, 874 F. Supp. at 1318.
Footnote: See 15 U.S.C. § 1692k
(governing civil liability under the
Act).

**Cushman v. Trans Union Corp.,
920 F. Supp. 80 (E.D. Pa. 1996) or
Cushman v. Trans Union Corp., 115
F.3d 220 (3d Cir. 1997)** - TransUnion
found liable.

**Richardson v. Fleet Bank of
Massachusetts** – the court held
that the Fleet Bank failed to follow
reasonable procedures by relying
on creditors for accurate credit
information because the company
had reason to know of the dispute
between the consumer and the
company.

**Bryant v. TRW** – the Defendant
consumer reporting agency
unsuccessfully argued that, under
§607(b) of the FCRA, 15 U.S.C.
§1681 et seq., it was not liable as
a matter of law, for reports it issued
in good faith, and as a result of
inaccurate information provided
to it by Plaintiff's creditors. The
court held that Defendant was not

free from liability when the credit reports at issue was not accurate. Once inaccuracy was determined, defendant's agency procedures were determined to be not reasonable to ensure maximum possible accuracy, pursuant to §§607(b).

## Damages

In **Bryant v. TRW, Inc., 487 F.Supp. 1234, 1242-43 (E.D.Mich.1980)**, the district court awarded a consumer $8,000 for anguish resulting from denials of a mortgage due to inaccurate credit reports. The Sixth Circuit affirmed. 689 F.2d 72 (6th Cir.1982).

**Fischl v. General Motors Acceptance Corp., 708 F.2d 143, 151 (5th Cir.1983).** – Actual damages include humiliation or mental distress, even if the consumer has suffered no out-of-pocket losses.

In **Pinner, 805 F.2d at 1265**, the consumer was awarded $25,000 for mental distress because of the humiliation and embarrassment

---

**Marc** ⬚⬚⬚
15 mins

Two wins in court today!!

Just finished in court today. I had two cases. Both of the defendants settled! One defendant settled right away before the judge could hear the case. The other defendant wanted to play hard ball. The lawyer was "waiting for a call from his client" for like an hour. Something about he doesn't think the company can remove it from the report. So the judge decided he wanted to hear the case. 15 mins into my presentation of evidence, it was not going well for the attorney. So the attorney said your honor I think we can reach an agreement if I can just call my client. The judge gave him 10 mins. Presto! The lawyer came back in 10 mins and said his client would remove the tradeline completely!

Lessons I learned:

1. Use the actual credit report from the CB in addition to Credit karma or some other 3rd party reporting. I used credit karma reports as evidence that the company did not report within 30 days. The lawyer objected to these "reports" saying they were not actual credit reports and there for were "hearsay." Not a deal breaker but if we use the actual report it takes that argument away from them, and potentially losing some critical evidence in your case.

2. Have the statues in front of you. The judge said it's been a while since he read the specific statue I am referencing. So he asked for my copy (which conveniently highlighted the sections I was using from the book)

3. Be able to speak specifically about the monetary harm. The judge asked how did you get the number $5,000 and what was my actual harm. I stated that each time they reported my information it can be a $1,000 fine, but beyond that I have lost out on two homes I wanted to purchase (one with $40,000 in equity and one with $15,000 in equity). So my actual harm could be $55,000. And the rate on my car loan is higher as well. But I was only asking for $5,000.

3. Always ask for money as part of the initial settlement negotiation. If you don't put it on the table up front it's hard to add it on later. Also note if you ask for $1,000 they will most likely counter with less than that--like $500. Lesson start high and negotiate down.

Anyway, Today is a huge win! Two tradelines deleted!

◯ Love       💬 Comment

⬚⬚ You, Steve Solem, Kelly Felix and 4 others

---

resulting from three credit denials and from lengthy dealings with the credit bureau.

**Thompson v. San Antonio Retail Merchants Ass'n, 682 F.2d 509, 513-14 (5th Cir.1982).** – The consumer received $10,000 because of humiliation and embarrassment suffered from three denials of credit and from the fact that the credit bureau took several months to correct the credit report's inaccuracies.

In **Collins v. Retail Credit Co., 410 F.Supp. 924, 936 (E.D.Mich.1976)**, the court awarded a consumer $21,750 for embarrassment and humiliation.

In **Morris v. Credit Bureau of Cincinnati, Inc., 563 F.Supp. 962, 969 (S.D.Ohio 1983)**, the consumer was awarded $10,000 for anguish and embarrassment even though, after he was denied credit, he explained the inaccuracies on his credit report and subsequently obtained credit.

Dana ███ ████
October 27, 2016

I'm not posted anything to this point but feel that I should because this is a big win. 4 years ago I had heart failure and almost lost everything needless to say my credit when in the trenches. Two and a half years ago I hired a credit repair company to help me get back online they did some help butt failed to get any response whatsoever from Portfolio Recovery Associates. So when I joined earlier this year I sent the first batch of letters off 4 of those were for accounts that Portfolio Recovery Associates again no response. The second set of letters went out with the same results no response. So I decided to go ahead and file a small claims lawsuit I didn't do it on all four of the accounts that they had but just the largest one which was only $800. They failed to respond so the case that filed for default. And they were sent default papers from the court they failed to file anything in proper time allotted for the default papers also. So this was being sent to the judge for signature for a $3,500 lawsuit. Today I got a call from an attorney representing the company. And wanted to negotiate. I told him that I would waive the $3,500 lawsuit but they had to take all four of the accounts off of my credit not sell them to anyone and close them out forever. About a half hour later he called back and agreed!

👍 Like    💬 Comment

😊❤️👍 You, Ebony ███ ████, Steve Solem and 249 others

In **Millstone v. O'Hanlon Reports, Inc., 528 F.2d 829, 834-35 (8th Cir.1976)**, the Eighth Circuit upheld an award of $2,500 for mental anguish after an insurer canceled the consumer's policy because of an inaccurate credit report.

## Advisory Opinion to Darcy (06-30-00)

June 30, 2000

Denise A. Darcy, Esq.
Asst. General Counsel
TRANS UNION
555 West Adams Street
Chicago, Illinois 60661

Dear Ms. Darcy:

This responds to your letter dated concerning whether the Fair Credit Reporting Act ("FCRA") allows Trans Union or another consumer reporting agency ("CRA"), for security purposes, to "truncate, scramble or mask the account number and social security number" when making file disclosures to consumers. You report that such a procedure has been recommended to you by a consumer who was recently the victim of account takeover fraud by a perpetrator who fraudulently procured the individual's Trans Union file by impersonating the consumer. You state: "While some creditors truncate or scramble the data before they supply it to us, not all do, therefore, many of the account numbers on our file are complete and accurate, and that is what we disclose to the consumer."

Section 609(a)(1) of the FCRA states that CRAs, including major credit bureaus such as Trans Union, "shall, upon request (by a consumer), clearly and accurately disclose to the consumer . . . *All information* in the consumer's file at the time of the request" (emphasis added). If the "information in the consumer's file at the time of the request" includes account and social security numbers, the provision thus normally requires that the CRA "clearly and accurately" include such items in its disclosure to consumers. However, because the trigger for a file disclosure is a "request" by a consumer, a CRA may allow consumers (such as the individual in your letter) to choose truncation or other security measures in their own file disclosure. In other words, although Section 609 provides consumers with a right to *all information* in the file, a CRA may provide a method for the consumer to ask for less than all information and then comply with that "request" when it makes the disclosure.

In sum, it is our view that a CRA that always scrambles or truncates account (or social security) numbers does not technically comply with Section 609 because it does not provide "accurate" (and perhaps not "clear") disclosure of "all information" in the file. However, if a consumer's "request" for a file disclosure is framed so as to allow some items in the file to be abbreviated or revised in that fashion, a CRA making such a disclosure would comply with Section 609.

The opinions set forth in this informal staff letter are not binding on the Commission.

Sincerely yours,

Clarke W. Brinckerhoff

# Finding a Registered Agent

A registered agent is a responsible third-party who is registered in the same state in which a business entity was established. A registered agent is also the person who will receive service of process notices, notice of lawsuits, correspondence from the Secretary of State, and other official government notifications. Sometimes these terms: registered agents, statutory agents, resident agents, service of process agents, and corporate agents are all used to designate the same thing.

The bottom line is that a registered agent exists to be available during certain business hours to accept service of process on behalf of a corporate entity, the first procedural step for filing a lawsuit. This is the address you will use to serve the creditor, collection agency, or credit bureau that you are suing in small claims court.

You can look up any registered agent of any corporate entity by doing a business name search online or by using a site such as **http://www.registeredagentinfo.com**

Choose which state you reside in, and then search the business name in the box provided. You may have to start with a small portion of the name in order to drill down to the exact business

---

When filing suit against a credit bureau, some folks have reported success by sending a copy of the lawsuit directly to a high-up person at the related credit bureau, as well as the Consumer Financial Protection Bureau.

CC:
Anthony Alexis
Assistant Director of Enforcement
Consumer Financial Protection Bureau
1700 G. Street NW
Washington, D.C. 2055

Equifax Corporation
Julie Shirley
SVP and Deputy General Counsel
Office of the General Counsel
1550 Peachtree St
NE Atlanta, GA 30309

Daniel Halvorsen
TransUnion Corp.
Sr. Attorney GROUP General Counsel
Office of the General Counsel
555 W. Adams Street
Chicago IL 60661

Experian North America
Ann Sterling
Vice President and Assistant General Counsel
Office of the Corporate Counsel
475 Anton Blvd.
Costa Mesa, CA 92626

best advised to get an attorney. You can do a search online for "FCRA attorney" or "FDCPA attorney" plus the name of your state, in order to find someone who can help you. Many of those types of lawyers do not charge a fee unless they win or get the other side to settle.

Or you can go to **http://www.creditsecret.org/legalshield**

entity. For example, Transunion's exact business name is "TRANS UNION LLC" so sometimes it is trial and error to get the correct registered agent.

Once you find the registered agent you will send a certified letter to that registered agent at their registered office address, or hire a process server to hand deliver your notice or complaint to them.

Now keep in mind that sometimes you may not be able to find their registered agent, and the defendant may not have a location in your state. A handful of small claims courts may not allow you to sue without that information. In that unlikely event, you may need to consider filing in district court, and for that you would be

You should have a good opportunity to file locally based on the Fair Debt Collection Practices Improvement Act of 1999: Most courts have held that FDCPA litigation is appropriately filed within the district where the consumer received the communication. Officers and managers of the debt collector who

have control over the procedures complained of may also be sued there. Filing in the district where the letter was received has been upheld even where the debt collector's letter had been forwarded to a district in which it did not do business.

Another tactic we've seen occasionally is that a defendant may try to get your lawsuit moved from small claims court over to federal court if you are suing based on the FCRA or FDCPA which are both federal laws. In that event, you may want to edit your suit, or just be prepared in advance, by additionally suing for a "state" law that is very similar to the federal law. Each state has its own laws that are very similar to the FCRA and FDCPA. You can do

a search online for "debt collection laws in my state" or "credit reporting laws in my state", and add those to your complaint if you desire. You can either do it when you file, or amend your suit later if the defendant tries to move it to federal court. Just keep in mind that this is a rare occurrence.

## Member Stories

Here is another way one of our members kept a lawsuit in his local court:

 P▆▆▆▆▆▆ What makes it all good to sue LOCALLY ...is that you sent a letter of dispute from your address ( state) and they usually respond- to you back at your address- therefore; the claim is allowable because in the process of them failing in marking item disputed( 99.9) YOU were injured..because you lost opportunity because your credit sucked so bad you couldn't get any good credit with low interest rates or a home loan. ANNNNNNNNNDDDD because TO dispute is your right under FCRA they are held liable under it and the FDCPA..in smalls claims in your local court.. I argued this against a change of venue to arbitration by the original contract...and the Judge agreed with me...as such that We start our Dispute in our house/our address, The issue becomes How they are REPORTING rather than the DEBT they suppose we owe......they come face us for Violation of FCRA.

Unlike · Reply · 👍 1 · 4 hrs · Edited

# ChexSystems Removals

ChexSystems is the "credit bureau" for checking accounts. Most people typically never hear about ChexSystems until they've been denied a new bank account or they aren't allowed to write a check at the store. ChexSystems is a consumer reporting agency (CRA) that tracks your checking and savings account activity. About 80 percent of all financial institutions across the United States use ChexSystems data for

See the table below for a summary of the information that banks and merchants report to ChexSystems, and how long it remains on your report.

| Activity | Description | When It's Deleted |
|---|---|---|
| Involuntary Account Closure | Bank closes your account usually "for cause" (e.g., writing too many bad checks or fraud) | After 5 years (unless you successfully dispute the listing or the bank or ChexSystems deletes the listing sooner) |
| Bounced Checks and/or Overdrafts | Usually for multiple instances | |
| Unpaid Negative Balances | Usually for outstanding overdraft/nonsufficient funds (NSF) fees or other charges | |
| Savings Account, Debit Card or ATM Abuse | For risky or dishonest behavior (e.g., depositing empty envelopes at ATM or frequently exceeding transfer limit) | |
| Outstanding Checks in SCAN Database of Returned Checks & Instances of Fraud | Checks issued or sent to a collection agency; returned or fraudulent checks | |
| Suspected Fraud or Identity Theft | For altering checks or providing false information on an application | |
| Inquiries | Initiated by you, a bank, an employer, a creditor, or other "permitted" party | After 90 days or no more than 3 years if initiated by you; otherwise after 5 years |
| Lost Checks & Debit Cards | | After 5 years (except check-ordering and application histories and unless you successfully dispute the listing or the bank or ChexSystems deletes the listing sooner) |
| Check-Ordering History from Past 3 Years | Routine reporting (not necessarily negative information but can indicate possible fraud) | |
| Number of Accounts Applied for in Past 90 Days | | |
| Social Security Number/ Driver's License Validation and/or Verification | | |

screening your applications. Others use a similar service called TeleCheck. If your application for a checking account gets rejected, it means there is a negative record on your checking account history.

## Are You In ChexSystems?

ChexSystems maintains a database of individuals who have written some bad checks, have overdrafted their account for too long, etc. Once you get on their list, you won't be able to open a checking account at most banks in the United States.

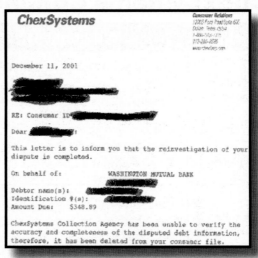

To make matter worse, there is no standard definition as to what constitutes "fraud" or "account abuse," according to the National Consumer Law Center. ChexSystems won't distinguish whether you were the victim or the perpetrator if there is a "suspected fraud" mark on your report.

## Correcting Errors In ChexSystems

If you believe you have erroneous, unverifiable, or unfair information in your ChexSystem record, you can follow the very same steps as in chapter 2. When preparing your letters, the bank that reported you to

ChexSystems can be considered the "creditor", and ChexSystems can be considered the "credit bureau".

## How To Get A Copy Of Your ChexSystems Report

Under the Fair Credit Reporting Act (FCRA), you are entitled to a free copy of your report once every 12 months or if you've been rejected by a bank in the past 60 days.

### Did you know?

ChexSystems must adhere to the FCRA - just like the other credit bureaus. Therefore similar letters can be used - i.e. P1L1 to the bank itself, and P2L1 to ChexSystems

# ChexSystems Continued

| Method | Requirement | Contact Info |
|---|---|---|
| **Online**<br>(Report Only) | Complete an Online Request Form<br>https://www.consumerdebit.com/<br>consumerinfo/us/en/chexsystems/report/<br>index.htm | consumerdebit.com |
| **By Phone**<br>(Report Only) | Follow the instructions of the<br>automated system | 800-428-9623 |
| **By Fax**<br>(Report Only) | Print and complete an Order Form<br>https://www.consumerdebit.com/<br>consumerinfo/us/en/Printable%20Order%20<br>Form.pdf | 602-659-2197 |
| **By Mail**<br>(Report or<br>Score) | **For Report:** Print and complete an<br>Order Form<br>https://www.consumerdebit.com/<br>consumerinfo/us/en/Printable%20Order%20<br>Form.pdf<br><br>**For Score:** Print and complete a<br>Score Order Form<br>https://www.consumerdebit.com/<br>consumerinfo/us/en/chexsystems/disclosure/<br>InquiryForm.pdf<br><br>Enclose a check/money order for<br>$10.50<br>made payable to ChexSystems, Inc. | ChexSystems, Inc.<br>Attn: Consumer<br>Relations<br>7805 Hudson Rd.,<br>Ste. 100<br>Woodbury, MN<br>55125 |

### Pro Tip: Check Your Information!

You have the right to dispute any information contained in your consumer file at ChexSystems.

ChexSystems must adhere to the FCRA - just like the other credit bureaus. Therefore similar letters can be used - i.e. P1L1 to the bank itself, and P2L1 to ChexSystems

Keep a copy for your files and send the letter registered mail.

---

Your Name
Your Address
City, State Zip

ChexSystems
Customer Relations
7805 Hudson Road, Suite 100
Woodbury, MN  55125

RE: Your SSN

Date:

To Whom It May Concern:

My bank has informed me that there is negative information reported by [insert name of bank] included in the file ChexSystems maintains under my Social Security Number. Upon ordering a copy of the report, I see an entry from this bank listing [insert reason for denial and date]. Please validate this information with [insert name of bank] and provide me with copies of any documentation associated with [insert reason for denial]. In the absence of any such documentation bearing my signature, I ask that this information be immediately deleted from the file you maintain under my Social Security Number.

Sincerely,

Your Signature
Your Name

---

# Dealing with Student Loans

If you defaulted on your student loans, you should also know that there is not a statute of limitations on student loan debt. Your loan company can keep trying to collect forever. Bankruptcy does not erase student loans either.

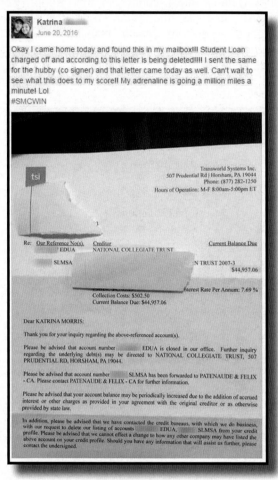

Many of our members have been successful with removing student loans from their credit report, that are reporting negatively. For this you would use Part 2 Letter 1 in Chapter 2

Depending on your circumstances, you might be able to get your payments deferred, get a forbearance agreement from your lender, consolidate your loans, or work your way through a process called loan rehabilitation.

## Deferment/ Forbearance

Both deferment and forbearance provide temporary relief, letting you suspend your payments for a specified period of time. They are not the same and if you decide to go this route you will prefer deferment if you qualify.

## Deferment

With deferment, as with forbearance, interest will continue to accrue during the time frame that you suspend your payments.

However, if you defer a federally subsidized student loan (a Federal Perkins Loan, a Direct Subsidized Loan, or a Subsidized Federal Stafford Loan), then the government pays the interest during this time period and it is not added back to the principal later on. This is why you want deferment for these types of loans.

## Forbearance

If you don't qualify for a deferment (you're not enrolled at an accredited school or unemployed) you still might be able to suspend your payments for a period of time by applying to your lender for forbearance.

Under some circumstances, your lender will be required to grant forbearance:

- You're in a medical or dental school residency program,

- Monthly student loan payments total more than 20% of your gross monthly income,

- You are involved in national or community service,

- You're teaching in a qualifying education program

- You're in the National Guard and you've been called up.

If you don't meet one or more of these conditions, you still might be able to get a forbearance; but your lender will have some discretion to say no, or to agree to suspend only a part of your monthly payment.

The main thing to remember about forbearance is that unlike deferment, you are responsible for interest during the payment suspension period. This interest can either be paid during forbearance, or it gets added onto the principal, not only increasing

**Bryan T**
May 11, 2015

My Lowest Score Went Up 100 points in last week and a half. Every student loan I EVER had including the federal ones owed to the government came off...It looks like I never even went to college. LOL!

# Student Loans Continued

your balance, but also the length of time it will take to pay off your loans.

If you want to learn more about both of these situations, visit this link: **http://studentaid. ed.gov/repay- loans/deferment- forbearance**.

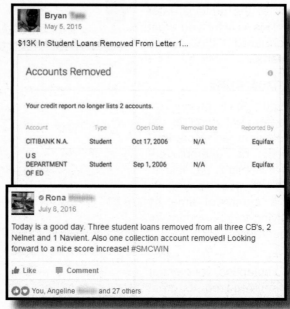

## Consolidation

This is a great option if you have more than one student loan, and the combined total of all your monthly payments is more than you can handle.

### Advantages to consolidating

1. You'll have a single monthly payment that is lower than the total of the payments you're making now.

### Pro Tip: Do You Qualify for Loan Forgiveness?

There are certain situations where you can have your federal student loan forgiven, canceled, or discharged. Find out whether you qualify due to your job, disability, the closure of your school, or other circumstances. Visit: **https://studentaid.ed.gov/sa/repay- loans/forgiveness-cancellation**

2. You might be able to extend the repayment period, resulting in a lower monthly payment.

3. You might be able to lock down a single, fixed rate if you are not in one already.

4. Flexible repayment plans are available.

5. Most types of student loan are eligible, both subsidized and unsubsidized.

# Vehicle Repossession

Make sure you have copies of all the documents related to your vehicle's purchase, as well as any repossession notices.

This includes (but is not limited to):

- The original retail installment sales contract;
- All documents provided by the dealer and lender;
- All correspondence from the dealer and lender, including envelopes;
- All documents relating to car repairs;
- All inspection documents; and
- All payments on the car loan.

Lisa
January 11

#SMCWIN - HAPPY NEW YEAR CREDIT FAMILY!!

I am wrapping up my journey here but I'm sure I'll hang out and offer advice where I can and continue to improve my score with higher limits on my cards and longer histories (YOUR CREDIT JOURNEY IS NEVER OVER!!) but here's the very recent update on my many wins:

1. CURRENT FICO - 720. Six months ago when I started here, it was in the low 600s.

2. . NEGOTIATED PAY FOR DELETE ON A COLLECTION - Fjled small claims with a debt collector, settled at less than .25 on the dollar.

3. BARCLAY CARD- $1300 limit

4. ULTA MC - $2000 limit

5. AMAZON CARD - $3900 limit

6. NORDSTROMS - $5000 limit

7. BLOOMINGDALES- $500 limit

8. OFFER FROM SANTANDER TO REMOVE CAR REPO TRADE LINE - Negotiatiating with them a time frame on when they can resell the debt.

9. REMOVAL OF BARNEY'S LATE PAYMENT - This was after all the letters, after a complaint with the CPFB was moved to the FDIC.

I still have late payments with JCrew and Navient, that's it. I'm not that optimistic about winning either of these honestly. Might fight, might just let it be. Late payments after 2 years are not that big of a deal.

These wins are in addition to the West Elm, Overstock, ZGallerie, Ann Taylor and Brylane Cards I got with the SHOPPING CART TRICK when I started.

THE WHOLE REASON I DID THIS - Since my Santander repo 18 months ago, I haven't had a car (IN LA!!) My goal here was always to walk into a dealership and get the lease they offer on television!!! Haha, will def send a picture of that car when I get it.

So grateful for this program. Stay fierce and fight the good fight. xx Lisa

You, Scott          , Steve Solem and 79 others          15 Comments

Love     Comment

You may need these documents in the case of any legal claims you could potentially establish against the car dealer and the lender, or to defend yourself against their possible lawsuits.

**Please remember:** a lender does not have to warn you before taking your car. If they do this, without going to court, it's called *self-help* repossession.

**Note:** The only exception is for cars owned by active duty service members. Active duty service members who have made at least one payment on a car loan cannot be subject to a lender's self-help repossession.

When the lender repossesses your car, it must do so without breaching the peace. When courts review a repossession to determine if a breach of peace occurred, they will look at whether the owner was present, whether the repo company entered the home or garage without the permission of the owner, and whether the repo company used force or the threat of violence to repossess the car. It is generally illegal if the lender repossessed the car while it was parked in a locked garage. If the court decides that the lender breached the peace, the lender and/or the repossession company will be liable for damages caused by the wrongful repossession.

## What does the lender have to do after the car is repossessed?

After repossession, the lender must provide two written notices.

## First Notice: Redemption

This notice must be provided to the owner of the car and all co-buyers or co-signers. It states that the lender has the car in its possession and that the car will be sold to recover the amount owed. This Notice of Sale may be the first written notice from your creditor after they repossess the vehicle, if you waived your right to notice of acceleration or if your state does not have a "right to cure" law. If you do not take action to recover your vehicle back before it is sold, then you will not be able to get it back.

The lender must send you this notice at least 10 days before the proposed sale of the car. The timing may be different in some states. This gives you a reasonable amount of time to get your car back. This usually means paying off the loan in full plus the lender's repossession costs.

The notice will contain information as to where you can get the exact payoff number it will take to get your vehicle back. The notice must be accurate about everything to do with your vehicle and the loan, and in most jurisdictions, it is required to state whether the sale will be open to the public or private, and where it will be.

If a creditor fails to send the you proper notice of the sale, then it is possible that a court will bar the debtor from collecting on a deficiency judgement, even if you know about the sale from an outside source. In some cases, the courts could force the creditor to pay you penalties because of an inadequate selling price.

Your right to redeem, or get your car back, lasts until the car is resold. The

**Lisa** 😊 feeling excited.
January 26 · Los Angeles, CA

#SMCWIN - Just negotiated $500 pay for delete w Santander for my car repo!!!

Steve Solem, Kelly Felix and 65 others          16 Comments

Like          Comment

letter will also state where and when the car will be sold, and if it is open to the public or is a private sale. If you want, you could attention the auction and bid on your own car. In some instances, re-purchasing the vehicle this way could be cheaper. Also, even though you still owe the lender money, which they can pursue via other legal means, they cannot threaten repossession any more.

## Second Notice: Deficiency

After your car is sold, the lender is then required to send out a second notice, stating the amount that the lender credited you from the resale, as well as a cancellation notice of the original sales contract. The majority of the time, cars are sold at wholesale auctions, at a much lower price than fair market value. If you feel a lender did this when reselling your vehicle, you might be able to use that to defend the "deficiency action" that they will file against you to recoup the difference in the sales price of the vehicle, and what

you owe the lender.

For example, in New Jersey, your claim against the lender will be that The Uniform Commercial Code, N.J.S.A. 12A: 9-610(b), whereas the lender is not entitled to all of the money it seeks because the sale was not *commercially reasonable* and, as a result, the sale price was unreasonably low. If your claim is successful, the court will award damages, under N.J.S.A. 12A:9-625, which will reduce or eliminate the amount you owe.

Each state is different and you will need to research the exact code to use.

Another way to reduce the amount due is to challenge the accuracy of this second notice because it may state that you owe more than you are

### Did you know?

Sometimes, filing for bankruptcy can prevent repossession? While the bankruptcy is pending, you can even pay off the car in full or catch up with any past-due payments.

supposed to. If you had any kind of gap insurance, or a service contract factored into the original purchase, those amounts should have been deducted from the amount that the lender states you owe.

## Filing For Bankruptcy Can Prevent Repossession

In general, if you file for bankruptcy, and if you qualify for an automatic stay, then creditors have to stop all collection efforts. This also means that the lender cannot repossess your car unless the bankruptcy court permits it. While the bankruptcy is pending, you can even pay off the car in full or catch up with any past-due payments.

## Car Dealer and Lender Must Follow Certain Laws

These laws include:

- Uniform Commercial Code
- Retail Installment Sales Act
- Truth in Lending Act
- Consumer Fraud Act

If these laws are not followed, you may have legal claims and defenses against the lender. Also, you may have claims against the dealer and the repo company.

But let's assume the reason you're here is to get a repo off of your credit report, instead of learning the vast laws about repo's. In that case, here are some letters that could help you.

# Repo Letter 1

Send to Collection Agency, Original Creditor, and Car Dealership.

Your Name
Your Address

Collection Agency Name & Address
Original Creditor Name & Address

Car Dealer Name & Address
Date

RE: VIN # [insert vin # here]

To Whom It May Concern,

This letter is a formal statement notifying the above parties that the accounts under VIN # [insert VIN # here] are disputed.

The vehicle in question was purchased on or about [insert date], financed by [insert company], repossessed in the state of [insert state], and sold by [insert insert company/creditor] on or about [insert date].

Under the laws of [insert state] and UCC § 9.506 as well as State RISA and MVISA statutes, a deficiency can not be claimed unless all of the required notices were properly and timely given, and all of the allowable redemption and cure time limits were adhered to.

I demand proof that the repossession of the subject vehicle was legal in accordance with the following UCC:

• § 9-506. EFFECT OF ERRORS OR OMISSIONS.

• § 9-611. NOTIFICATION BEFORE DISPOSITION OF COLLATERAL

• § 9-612. TIMELINESS OF NOTIFICATION BEFORE DISPOSITION OF COLLATERAL.

• § 9-613. CONTENTS AND FORM OF NOTIFICATION BEFORE DISPOSITION OF COLLATERAL

You are required to provide me with copies of the legal notices and proof of the commercially reasonable manner of the notification and resale of the subject vehicle.

If no such proof is provided within 15 days from receipt of this certified mail notice, the alleged claim of a deficiency will be considered null and void, and any continued collection activities, or continued reporting of this invalid claim on my credit reports will be considered a violation of the FDCPA and FCRA.

In addition, if you singularly or severally fail to comply with the above

*(Letter continued on next page)*

*(Repo Letter 1 continued)*

requests, I reserve the right to seek damages against all parties, under all available State and Federal statutes and including but not limited to UCC § 9-625 remedies.

Furthermore, you are hereby notified that at no point in time and under no circumstances is your company; an employee of your company; a representative for your company or affiliates are to contact me or any family members by any means other than the US mail system.

Your Name (printed or typed, not signed)
SSN
Address

Cc: Consumer Financial Protection Bureau
Cc: Attorney General's Office
Cc: Better Business Bureau

# Repo Letter 2

Send to Credit Bureaus after 15 days of sending Repo Letter 1.

Your Name
Your Address

Credit Bureau Name
Credit Bureau Address
Date

RE: SSN # [insert SSN # here]

This letter is in reference to the account listed on my credit report by [insert company name] under account # [insert acct #]. This account is being illegally reported on my credit report. I formally disputed it directly with [insert company name] in regards to their illegal reporting, and have not received any satisfactory reply.

Therefore, I am now formally disputing directly with you. Furthermore, if at any time during your investigation the above account is verified by [insert company name] I am requesting your method of verification pursuant to the FCRA, including the name of the person with whom you spoke, who has firsthand knowledge of the account in question.

I am maintaining a careful record of my communications with you for the purpose of filing a complaint with the Consumer Financial Protection Bureau and the Attorney General's office, should you continue reporting this erroneous item.

Your Name (printed or typed, not signed)

P.S. Please be aware that dependent upon your response, I may be detailing any potential issues with your company via an online public press release.

Cc: Consumer Financial Protection Bureau
Cc: Attorney General's Office
Cc: Better Business Bureau

**Nina**
January 30

Great news for my brother who I have been helping with his credit since November. I disputed his repo and a sprint account. After pulling his credit report from Equifax, his repo is GONE and sprint too!!!! He is so happy! His score jumped up 65 points! This book is amazing and I'm grateful for the people that have shared this amazing secret!

Kelly Felix, Stefan James and 55 others        6 Comments

Like        Comment

# HIPAA & Medical Collections

Do you have a collection agency harassing you about a medical bill? If so, what can sometimes happen, is you may send them Part 1, Letter 1 from Chapter 2 of this book, and in return they send you a copy of a medical bill that they claim is yours.

Typically the following also happens:

a) They show <u>no proof</u> that they have an agreement with the original creditor to collect this alleged debt

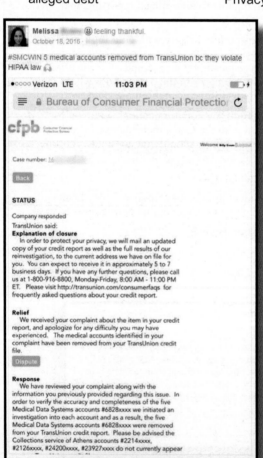

b) They have no copy of a signed contract where you allegedly agreed to pay the charges

c) The medical bill reveals personal medical information about you

While A or B are usually enough to give you the leverage you need to make them go away, C is the big one because it may put them in violation of HIPAA (Health Insurance Portability and Accountability Act of 1996). Privacy rules prohibit disclosing an individual's protected health information unless you specifically authorized them to.

*So if the doctor or hospital shared anything on the bill that alludes to your condition or what you may have been treated for, they may have just broken privacy rules.*

## This gives you LEVERAGE.

And that leverage makes you a problem for both the collection agency and the hospital/doctor. Usually it is a problem that they will all want to go away quickly, so that they can go after others who are not aware of these laws.

Here are some letters that could help with medical collections.

# Letter To Original
# Health Care Provider

Your Name
Address
City, State, Zip
SSN

HIPAA Compliance Office

Health care provider creditor
Address
Date

Dear Sir/Madam;

This letter is in reference to [account #] for services provided to [name of patient] on [date of service].

In regard to the bill on this account in the amount of $_____:

Please be advised that under Federal Statutes, The Fair Credit Reporting Act, (15 U.S.C. § 1681 et seq) and [name of your State]'s Consumer Credit Statutes, and subtitle D of the ARRA ,SEC. 13401. APPLICATION OF SECURITY PROVISIONS AND PENALTIES TO BUSINESS ASSOCIATES OF COVERED ENTITIES; and SEC. 13407(1) BREACH OF SECURITY.

The term "breach of security" means, with respect to unsecured PHR identifiable health information of an individual in a personal health record, acquisition of such information without the authorization of the individual. You may be held liable for the actions of [collection agency name].

Please note that the these liabilities are under the penalty rules of the Omnibus Final Rule effective 09/23/2013 interpreting and implementing various provisions of the Health Information Technology for Economic and Clinical Health Act of 2009 (HITECH Act) as issued 11/30/2009

   *(a) Duty of furnishers of information to provide accurate information.*
   *(1) Prohibition.*
   *(A) Reporting information with actual knowledge of errors.*

HIPAA and [name of your State]'s Medical Privacy Statutes and the penalty provisions of the ARRA section D, privacy provisions ,the penalty rules of the HITECH Act as issued 11/30/2009 and the Omnibus Final Rule effective 09/23/2013 and the FACT Act final rules effective July 1, 2010 are in effect in this situation.

The Privacy Rules prohibits a covered entity from using or disclosing an individual's protected health information ("PHI") unless specifically

*(Letter continued on next page)*

*(Letter to original healthcare provider continued)*

authorized by the individual or otherwise allowed under the Privacy Rules.

In general, PHI encompasses substantially all "individually identifiable health information" that is transmitted or maintained in any medium. "Individually identifiable health information" includes health information that is created or received by a health care provider, health plan, employer, or health care clearinghouse, and that relates to an individual's physical or mental health or condition, including information related to an individual's care or the PAYMENT for such care.

Your furnishing of my account information to [collection agency name], is not in compliance with HIPAA,or [name of your State]'s Privacy Act, and any subsequent reporting of this account on my credit reports to [credit reporting bureaus] is a clear violation of Public Law 104-191 ("HIPAA").

I am requesting you promptly rescind all such account information furnished to [collection agency] and require them to purge their records of all reference to this account, and that you insure that any and all reporting of this account is immediately deleted from my credit reports.

*(insert the underlined phrase for hospitals)*

You are also advised that you may be in violation of the Notice of Proposed Procedures for Charitable Hospitals to Correct and Disclose Failures to Meet Section 501(r) of the Affordable Care Act.

Please respond, in writing within 10 days acknowledging that you are processing this request.

I am reserving the right, to take appropriate legal and civil action including reporting to any applicable regulatory authorities any lack of cooperation or compliance with this request.

I hereby waive my rights under HIPAA and any State Privacy Act for the single purpose of your transmission of this request and accompanying documentation in any required report you must make to your E &O insurance carrier.

Sincerely,

Name (printed not signed)

# HIPAA Collection Agency Validation, Dispute, Cease & Desist

This letter is to notify the agency that the debt is beyond SOL, or is invalid for other reasons, and subject to the HIPAA privacy laws.

---

Your Name
Your Address
Collection Agency Name
Collection Agency Address
Date

Re: Acct # XXXX-XXXX-XXXX-XXXX

To Whom It May Concern:

This letter is being sent to you in response to your recent letter.

This is not a refusal to pay, but a notice that your claim is disputed.

Under the Fair Debt Collections Practices Act (FDCPA), I have the right to request validation of the debt you say I owe you. I am requesting proof that I am indeed the party you are asking to pay this debt,the date of the alleged medical service, the name of the patient, and proof that there is some contractual obligation which is binding on me to pay this debt.

Please attach copies of:

Any agreement with your client that grants you the authority to collect on this alleged debt, or proof of acquisition by purchase or assignment, and authorization under subtitle D of the ARRA, SEC. 13401. APPLICATION OF SECURITY PROVISIONS AND PENALTIES TO BUSINESS ASSOCIATES OF COVERED ENTITIES; and SEC. 13407(1) BREACH OF SECURITY.

The term "breach of security" means, with respect to unsecured PHR identifiable health information of an individual in a personal health record, acquisition of such information without the authorization of the individual.

Please note that enforcement of penalties against you is covered under the penalty rules of the Omnibus Final Rule effective 09/23/2013 interpreting and implementing various provisions of the Health Information Technology for Economic and Clinical Health Act of 2009 (HITECH Act) as issued 11/30/2009 and the penalty rules of the FCRA and FACTA including FACT Act changes final rules effective July 1, 2010.

---

*(Letter continued on next page)*

*(Validation, Dispute, Cease & Desist Letter continued)*

<u>Please also attach</u> copies of any agreement that bears the signature of the alleged debtor wherein he or she agreed to pay the creditor and as this is a medical account a copy of any HIPAA authorization.

Please also be advised that this letter is not only a formal dispute, but a request that you cease and desist any and all collection activities, including reporting of; or verifying of this account on my credit reports.

I require compliance with the terms and conditions of this letter within 30 days. or a complete withdrawal, in writing, of any claim.

In the event of noncompliance, I reserve the right to file charges and/ or complaints with the OCR on your HIPAA violations and appropriate County, State & Federal authorities, the CFPB, BBB and State Bar associations for violations of the FDCPA, FCRA, and Federal and State statutes on illegal collection activities on any account that may be time-barred as well as in violation of [name of your State] medical privacy rules.

I also hereby reserve my right to take private civil action against you to recover damages.

Sincerely,

Name (printed not signed)

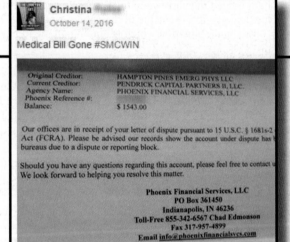

Christina
October 14, 2016

Medical Bill Gone #SMCWIN

Original Creditor:          HAMPTON PINES EMERG PHYS LLC
Current Creditor:         PENDRICK CAPITAL PARTNERS II, LLC.
Agency Name:             PHOENIX FINANCIAL SERVICES, LLC
Phoenix Reference #:
Balance:                 $ 1543.00

Our offices are in receipt of your letter of dispute pursuant to 15 U.S.C. § 1681s-2 Act (FCRA). Please be advised our records show the account under dispute has bureaus due to a dispute or reporting block.

Should you have any questions regarding this account, please feel free to contact We look forward to helping you resolve this matter.

Phoenix Financial Services, LLC
PO Box 361450
Indianapolis, IN 46236
Toll-Free 855-342-6567 Chad Edmonson
Fax 317-957-4899
Email info@phoenixfinancialsvcs.com

Christopher
40 mins

Well this program works for sure the new smart money secret I got one of the new accounts it's shows a balance and of 53 and a credit limit of 5000 score jumped up 45 points utilization went from 74% to 41% awesome WIN WIN

# Good Credit Lines Quickly

## Method 1: Alternative Credit Cards and Credit Lines

Would you like to get $10,000 in guaranteed credit added to your credit report without a credit check?

You can do so right here:
http://creditsecret.org/secret-money-method

What's the benefit of getting more credit if your score is in the dumps?

As we explained earlier in this book, 30% of your score is determined by amounts owed, and 10% is determined by new credit.

So let's say you currently have a $5,000 credit card limit and you owe $4,500 on it. That would mean you are at 90% usage. This dramatically hurts your FICO score.

By adding $10,000 in new credit, you would now only owe $4,500 on $15,000 available credit, bringing your utilization down from 90% to only 30%. In this case your FICO score would skyrocket. Additionally, since the $10,000 is "new credit" your score would again improve.

The goal of getting $10,000 in new credit is not to go and spend it - its main purpose is to show the credit bureaus that you are responsible and you aren't maxed out.

You can get $10k in guaranteed credit added to your credit report, without a credit check here:
http://creditsecret.org/secret-money-method

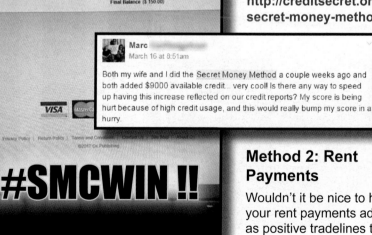

## Method 2: Rent Payments

Wouldn't it be nice to have your rent payments added as positive tradelines to your credit reports? Now you can.

Go to RentReporters **http://www.rentreporters.com** and use promo code: BA539 for $10 off

RentReporters reports your on-time rent payments to the credit bureau which will help increase your score.

## Method 3: Piggybacking

**Dave** ▓▓▓▓
March 14 at 12:55pm

#SMCWIN

I purchased the book and joined this group back in August 2016. I had 16 derogatory accounts and 2 Tax Liens and a Chapter 7 & Chapter 13 in the Public Record which was showing on all (3) CB's when I started. I READ THE BOOK SEVERAL times. I wanted to know that book like the back of my hand.

Today there is only 1 remaining derogatory account and I just filed in Small Claims on them and I suspect once they read my complaint that will collapse like the little bitches that they are. The BK;s and TL's have all been removed except the Cpt 7 on Equifax and 1 Tax Lien on Experian.

I had great success being sued years ago in court by Debt Collectors, I was sued 5 times and won all 5 cases. I knew how to defend myself in a court against them, I was pretty much a Bad-Ass when it came to that defense.

What I knew little about was how to restore my credit. I have not applied or used credit since 2008.

A few weeks ago the Credit Secret offered how to establish $10,000.00 of unsecured credit using their method. If I remember correctly it was a (1) time fee of $69.00 upgrade for the info. Already trusting those who developed the Credit Secret book and program I did NOT hesitate to purchase the upgrade. I immediately followed the directions of that "Secret Money Method" and it WORKED LIKE A CHARM. Within 30 days I had $10,000.00 in credit and my utilization when through the roof.

I was just approved for a $25,000.00 purchase with CarMax. Im a simple guy, I don't need fancy. I love what a mini van offers.

I want to publicly thank this Team and this group for their support, wisdom, determination and willingness to fight back against those who choose to lie, cheat and do harm to people and families.

In gratitude,
Dave

👍😍😮 You, Steve Solem, Kelly Felix and 243 others          78 Comments

♡ Love          💬 Comment

A friend of mine named Tyler moved to the U.S. from Canada and had no credit. He asked his friend with great credit to add him onto his Platinum Amex account as an "authorized user". Tyler never even used the card and 6 months later his credit was 720.

This is because he is taking advantage of his friend's great credit history. Tyler's friend vouched for him and the credit bureaus love that when it comes from a reputable person.

A lot of 18-22 year olds do the same thing, piggybacking on their parent's accounts. Spouses also help each other out this way if one has better credit than the other.

By doing this, the authorized user receives a spillover of benefits of the main account holder's good credit, without ever actually needing to use the card.

# The Shopping Cart Trick

Here is a little-known trick that allows people with bad credit to obtain a credit card. And in doing so, you increase your overall available credit on your credit report, and your score jumps as a result.

You see, this shopping cart trick relies on the fact that some websites pre-approve you when you add items to your online shopping cart, without actually checking your score. This shopping cart trick is what is known as a "soft pull" on your credit report.

If you are a member of our VIP Facebook group, the Smart Money Club, you can do a search using the term "shopping cart trick, " and you'll see countless posts of people who have gotten it to work for them!

There are a couple of rules we need to follow:

1. Make sure your pop-up blocker is turned off on your web browser. This could be important depending on the website. You just want to ensure you won't miss the offer. Plus, when you are done, you can turn it back on.

2. Only use the last part of your social security number. If they ask for all of the numbers in your SSN, do not complete the form. Try again later or on another website.

## Shopping Cart Trick Credit Opportunities

This list will provide you with several options that have been tested with the Shopping Cart List. Instead of hitting them all at one time, select two or three and focus on those before moving onto other offers.

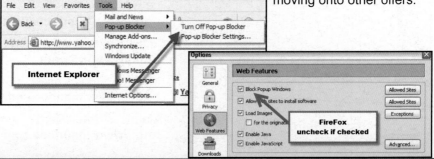

## Here is a list of the most popular cards.

Abercrombie & Fitch Credit Card
**https://abercrombie.com/shop/us**

Ann Taylor Credit Card
**http://www.anntaylor.com**

Avenue Credit Card
**http://www.avenue.com**

Bath & Body Works
**http://bathandbodyworks.com**

Bon Ton Credit Card
**http://www.bonton.com**

Boston Store Credit Card
**http://www.bostonstore.com**

Brylane Home Credit Card
**http://www.brylanehome.com**

Buckle Credit Card
**http://www.buckle.com**

Coldwater Creek
**http://www.coldwatercreek.com**

Crate and Barrel Credit Card
**https://www.crateandbarrel.com**

David's Bridal Credit Card
**http://www.davidsbridal.com**

Eddie Bauer Credit Card
**http://www.eddiebauer.com**

Express Credit Card
**http://www.express.com**

GameStop
**http://www.gamestop.com**

Home Shopping Network (HSN)
**http://www.hsn.com**

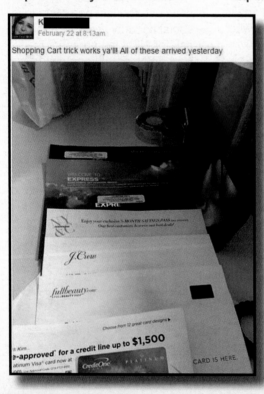

J.Crew
**http://www.jcrew.com**

J. Jill Credit Card
**http://www.jjill.com**

Jessica London
**http://jessicalondon.com**

Justice Credit Card
**http://shopjustice.com**

King Size Direct
**http://kingsizedirect.com**

Lane Bryant Credit Card
**http://lanebryant.com**

La Redoute Credit Card
**http://www.laredoute.com**

LOFT Credit Card
**http://www.loft.com**

Mandee Credit Card
**https://www.mandee.com**

Maurices Credit Card
**http://www.maurices.com**

Motorola
http://www.motorola.com

MyPoints
http://www.mypoints.com

New York & Co. Rewards
Credit Card
http://nyandcompany.com

Newport News Credit Card
http://www.spiegel.com/
newport-news

One Stop Plus
http://www.onestopplus.com

Overstock.com *(Be careful
with your social on this one!
Only enter last 4!)*
http://www.overstock.com

PacSun Credit Card
http://www.pacsun.com

Peebles/Stage Stores Credit Card
http://www.stage.com

Pier 1 Credit Card
http://www.pier1.com

Pottery Barn Kids Credit Card
http://www.potterybarnkids.com

Pottery Barn Credit Card
http://www.potterybarn.com

Restoration Hardware Credit Card
https://restorationhardware.com

Roamans
http://www.roamans.com

Spiegel Credit Card
http://www.spiegel.com

The Sportsman's Guide Visa
http://sportsmansguide.com

Steeles Credit Card
http://www.steeles.com

Talbots Credit Card
https://www.talbots.com

TigerDirect Credit Card
http://www.tigerdirect.com

Torrid Credit Card
http://www.torrid.com

Total Rewards
https://www.totalrewards.com

Venus Credit Card
http://www.venus.com

Victoria's Secret Credit Card
https://www.victoriassecret.com

Vitacost Rewards Mastercard
http://www.vitacost.com

Wayfair
http://www.wayfair.com

Woman Within Credit Card
http://www.womanwithin.com

## Here is your step-by-step process to do the Shopping Cart Trick:

1) Make sure your browser history, cookies and cache has all been cleared out. You will have to go into your browser settings to do this. This step is essential because the browser (and website) will have your information before you can give it to them.

2) Create a new account at the website you want to try to obtain a credit card. Usually, there is a place to create a free account or join their loyalty program in the top right area of the page. Enter everything about yourself as it appears on your credit report. Typically, Comenity Bank provides all of the above cards, and they use Experian. Just make sure your info matches up with theirs. You also want to subscribe to the store emails because sometimes they send pre-approvals to your email.

3) Go on a browsing spree and place a few items in your shopping cart. It seems to work best when you have a few products that total up to around $100. If it doesn't work right away, you can change it up or down by $50, as that seems to be the best option.

4) Start to check out. Navigate to your cart like you are going to purchase the items you added. Place all of the billing information it's asking for in the online form but type slowly. You don't want to use the autofill feature that your browser may provide.

5) Patience is to your advantage. If it's working correctly, a pop-up window will show up with a credit card offer. You will know it worked if it asks for the last four digits of your social security number.

6) Repeat the process. You can do this with as many cards as you wish. If it doesn't work right away, keep a lookout in your emails. You may also receive offers in your inbox over the next few days.

You do not have to purchase anything for this trick to work. Just know that

after you fill out your application, it will probably take you back to the checkout page. Once you are finished with the application, you can just abandon your shopping cart by closing the whole page down.

Initially, your credit cards may have very low credit limits of $500 or less. However some members have received as much as $2,500 per card.

This trick is useful to you if you currently have bad credit and need a way to add positive credit lines to your credit report without the hard pull (hard inquiry).

# Utilizing Credit Unions

One of the best credit unions to join is the Navy Federal Credit Union if you meet their membership criteria. They have fantastic rates on loans and credit cards, and free checking and savings accounts.

They've also been known to give high limit unsecured credit cards to people with bad credit.

Navy Federal primarily serves members with military affiliations - meaning someone in your immediate family has to have served in the military.

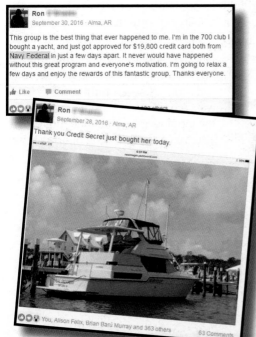

The BEST part about being a member of Navy Federal is that they give out HUGE credit limits to members, even with terrible credit. We recommend applying for their Visa Signature Rewards card in order to get the highest limit. We've even seen people with credit scores in the low 500's be approved for as much as $25,000.

Navy Federal is also great about loans as well. Some member have obtained a low-interest loan from them, and then used that to pay off other high interest debt.

But what if you don't have any relatives in the military? Skip to PenFed.org which we go over next. They are also an excellent credit union.

## Pentagon Federal

Anyone can join Pentagon Federal Credit Union. If you are not affiliated with the military, they ask you to donate a minimal amount to one of their charities or affiliations. As their website states: "Go to **PenFed.org** and choose Join PenFed. In three steps, you'll become a PenFed member."

First they'll ask for your eligibility. Just follow the prompts on the application and choose which organization to "join" and fulfill their requirements.

Then finish filling out all your personal information.

Then they will ask you to fund your account. When you open a credit union account you fund your "ownership" in that credit union. The minimum deposit for a PenFed Share Account is $5. Your membership fees to whichever organization you chose

in step one will also be added to the total. Remember: once you are a member of PenFed, you do not have to continue your membership in the qualifying organization you chose. Once a member, always a member.

Double check all your information and submit the application. You'll get confirmation right away. They will email you further instructions for logging into your account where you can see what they offer as far as

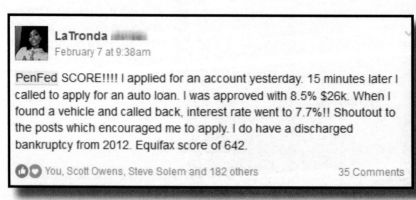

loans and credit cards.

## Points to Consider

When you open an account with PenFed, your Equifax credit report is pulled.

PenFed utilizes the same pull for 90 days for lending decisions. You can apply for all types of credit they offer within 90 days without a second inquiry performed.

Always apply by phone for products! Why? A few reasons. First, when you apply for a product online, there is an automated credit screening that is programmed to look for certain things on your CR (i.e. charge-offs, collections, high utilization rates, etc.). The automated system "reads" your CR and either spits out a denial or approval; if a denial, you'll get generic reasons, like the ones mentioned earlier - charge-offs, collection, too many

revolving accounts.

Also when you apply by phone, although the customer service rep you speak with is using the same system that would be used if you applied online, if you are denied, you can ask to be connected to a loan officer (LO) and explain your situation. Many times, the LO can push through (i.e. override) an application that was previously denied, and/or inform you what you do qualify for, and what you need to have removed from your credit report in order to qualify for the product you were looking for originally.

**Yolanda**
30 mins

One month ago yesterday, I posted here for advise on how to get a car because mine died...I was in tears and didn't know what to do next....But I thank God for this group!!!! I got some sound advice, keep on sending out my letters and praying for a miracle...In one month, I was approved for another credit card and an auto loan!!!! I brought this home yesterday!!!!!

**#SMCWIN !!**

♡ Love      💬 Comment

👍♡ You and 27 others

**Wilfred**
February 1

#Smcwin I got my BK deleted from equifax. I called penfed today for a personal loan to use it to travel. I got approved for $35,000!!! Thank you!!!

👍♡😊 Scott Owens, Steve Solem and 120 others

**Brian Barú Murray**
February 24 at 5:34pm

#smcwin Just got my wife approved for a Navy Federal Card for 14.8k

👍♡😊 Steve Solem, Dominique Davis and 98 others          14 Comments

**Denise**
February 6 at 9:19am

I know everyone raves about penfed (and kudos to those whom they've helped) but I have to applaud navy federal yet again.

This time it's my husband's #smswin

He has no collections. His repo is still on his credit report but it's showing paid in full. His credit usage is at 6%. His equifax score is 589. (He only has 3 trade lines reporting. Waiting for his auto loan to report.) Experian 659. Transunion 633

Cash rewards visa $7500! Checking line of credit $2000!

👍♡😊 You, Scott Owens, Steve Solem and 59 others          11 Comments

# Business Credit

If you run a business, or you want to run a business, then you will likely want to build a business profile. A lot of people fund their business dreams with their own personal credit history, but there is no reason to risk your personal credit history. Building business credit is as simple as following the steps below:

- Incorporate your business using a site like **http://LegalZoom. com** is a good option

- Obtain a federal tax identification number (EIN)

- Apply for a D-U-N-S® at **http://creditsecret.org/dnb**

- Open a business bank account

- Have a business phone number

- Ask For Trade References or tradelines

- Obtain business credit card(s)

- Establish a line of credit with vendors or suppliers

- Monitor Your Scores & Ratings

There are many ways to incorporate your business, and we won't get into which entity is best. You can visit **http://LegalZoom.com** and take care of the paperwork right online.

You'll apply for a federal EIN at the same time you incorporate.

Once you've done that, you'll want to apply for a D-U-N-S® number at **http://creditsecret.org/dnb**. D&B are a business credit agency, but they don't actually grant credit to businesses. What they do is provide businesses with the data to decide whether or not to extend a line of credit to another business.

A DUNS number is a nine-digit number that is unique to your company. This DUNs number will be used to create your business credit file, similar to how your social security number is used to identify your personal credit reports.

You'll need a bank account in the business name, as well as a phone number, and maybe a fax number. It's a good idea to have all these separate from any personal accounts.

## Business Credit Lines

### Kabbage
**http://creditsecret.org/kabbage**

- Sign up in minutes and get a decision instantly.
- No cost or obligation to draw funds.
- Take only what you need, when you need it.
- Pay only for only what you take.
- Access your cash 24/7.

Grow your business.

Another quality site for business credit info is **Creditsuite** **http://creditsecret.org/creditsuite**

Go there to get a free report on *"How to build credit for your EIN that's not linked to your SSN".*

# Credit Card for No Credit or Low Credit Scores

## Secured Cards

Secured cards are great for boosting your score and building positive payment history, as well as for increasing your credit limit to debt ratio. Basically you determine your account limit by how much you deposit. After several months of payment history, more opportunities can open up for unsecured credit lines.

### Primor Secured Mastercard
http://creditsecret.org/primor

Reports to all three nationwide credit bureaus. Approval up to $5000.

Those with a monthly income exceeding their monthly expenses by $100 or more are encouraged to apply.

### First Progress Platinum Prestige
http://creditsecret.org/prestige

- No Credit History or Minimum Credit Score Required for Approval
- Monthly Reporting to all 3 Major Credit Bureaus to Establish Credit History
- Credit Line Secured by Your Fully-Refundable Deposit of $200 -- $2,000 Submitted with Application

### Milestone MasterCard
http://creditsecret.org/milestone

- Pre-qualifying for the Milestone® Gold MasterCard® is quick and easy and will not affect your credit score.
- Free 24/7 Account Access & Bill Pay

### Open Sky Secured:
http://creditsecret.org/opensky

- Build Your Credit fast with our monthly reporting to all 3 major credit bureaus.
- Choose your credit line as low as $200 up to $3000, secured by a fully-refundable* security deposit.
- Security deposit needs to be submitted before the credit card can be issued.
- No credit check necessary and no checking account required; apply in less than 5 minutes.
- No credit history required to apply
- No fees for application and processing
- Accepted everywhere you see the Visa logo

### SelfLender.com
http://creditsecret.org/selflender

Self Lender also offers credit products to people with bad credit or no credit by offering Credit Builder Accounts. Credit Builder accounts help people who need to build their credit through installment loans.

A Credit Builder Account is like a reverse loan. You pay the payments first, and you get the money afterwards. The account is structured as a loan, and you build credit as you make payments towards your account. All of your loan payments are reported to all three credit bureaus.

## Merit Secured Card
**http://creditsecret.org/merit**

- Guaranteed $500 Unsecured Credit Limit card; no credit check, no employment check
- Reports to Major Bureau
- Fast Online Application

## Horizon Gold Card
**http://creditsecret.org/horizon**

- $500 Limit
- Easy Terms*
- No Credit Check
- No Employment Check
- Reports to Major Bureau
- Fast Online Application

## Group One Freedom Card
**http://creditsecret.org/freedom**

- $500 Limit
- Easy Terms*
- No Credit Check
- No Employment Check
- Reports to Major Bureau
- Fast Online Application

## Unsecured Cards

Indigo Mastercard
**http://creditsecret.org/indigo**

- All credit histories considered.
- Account history is reported to the three major credit bureaus.
- Quick Pre-Qualification (No Impact to your Credit Score).
- 60 Second Decision.
- Choose Your Custom Card Design – FREE.
- Mobile Account Access 24/7.

## Shopping Cards

Shopping cards allow you to get <u>unsecured credit lines</u> for use with online shopping at specific websites. As it relates to your credit score, it is less important to consider what type of shopping is offered, and more important to consider that you will get a credit score boost.

### NetFirst
**http://creditsecret.org/netfirst**

- $500 Limit
- Easy Terms*
- No Credit Check
- No Employment Check
- Reports to Major Bureau
- Fast Online Application

### Next Millennium
http://creditsecret.org/millennium

- ENJOY A $1,000.00 CREDIT LINE!
- 0% Financing on brand name products exclusively at our online store.
- Your Approval is Guaranteed!*
- Low Monthly Payments!
- No Credit Checks & No Credit Turndowns!

### Fingerhut
http://creditsecret.org/fingerhut

- All credit types welcome
- Start using your credit right away
- Low monthly payments
- Report payment history to the credit bureaus
- No annual fees, membership fees, or overlimit fees
- Shop over 550,000 items including brand names like Sony, Dell, LG, Keurig, Samsung, Shark, Adidas, and more.

### Soar Platinum
http://creditsecret.org/soar

- No Credit Check
- $1,000 unsecured
- No Application Denied for Bad Credit!
- Up to $1,000 Credit Line

*Comes with 2 Bonus Offers:*

1. **Prepaid Visa Card**

- No Credit Check
- Free Online Bill Pay
- No Overdraft Fees

2. **$500 Installment Loan**

- 2 Minute Approval Process
- Get Cash within 24 hours
- Poor Credit OK

## Auto Loans

### Boost Auto Loan
http://creditsecret.org/boost

Good Credit, Bad Credit, No Credit. Their partner dealer network extends throughout the USA. They can quickly assist in finding the right financing for any situation, with the right lender. Once your financial application has been verified, you can start looking for your vehicle.

### Web2Carz Auto
http://creditsecret.org/web2carz

- Acceptance In Minutes
- Nationwide Coverage
- Bad Credit, Previous Repossession, Bankruptcy OK

## Personal Loans

### Loanzi
http://creditsecret.org/loanzi

- Simple Online Process
- Get $500 to $35,000 in cash, direct deposited to your bank account in as little as one business day after approval.
- All Credit Types Welcomed

### 247Loan Express
http://creditsecret.org/247loan

- Dependable & reliable.
- Speedy approval. Get a response in 90 seconds or less.
- Borrow up to $35,000.
- No fuss, hassle free process.
- Cash as soon as the next business day.

### MyLoanz
http://creditsecret.org/myloanz

- Simple Online Process
- Get $500 to $35,000 in cash, direct deposited to your bank account in as little as one business day after approval.
- All Credit Types Welcomed

### Opp Loans
http://creditsecret.org/opploans

- Get approved quickly and receive money in your account as soon as the next business day.
- Lower Interest.
- Highly rated.
- Reports to credit bureaus.

### Guide to lenders
http://creditsecret.org/guide

Personal loans for 620 credit score or higher. Find a Personal Loan in 4 Easy Steps by comparing lenders matched to your specific needs.

## Debt Relief

### Debt Restructure
http://creditsecret.org/debt

- Answer a few questions online
- Get a free debt evaluation
- See how much you could save

### Accredited Debt Relief
http://creditsecret.org/accredited

- Free consultation
- Get out of debt without bankruptcy
- Resolve debt in as little as 24-48 months
- Get a free savings estimate
- No upfront fees & no obligation

## Mortgage Loans

### Low Rates Shop
http://creditsecret.org/lowrate

Look for multiple lenders that match your criteria for either refinancing an existing mortgage, or buying your first home.

## Student Loan Refinancing

### LendKey
http://creditsecret.org/lendkey

*Lower Your Payments.* You can reduce your interest rate, lower your monthly payments, and save thousands over the lifetime of your student loans.

*Simplify Your Finances.* You'll be able to refinance your federal and private student loans, including graduate loans, into one convenient loan at a great rate.

*Flexible Repayment Options.* Get personalized quotes with various repayment terms, including interest-only payments for the first four years.

*No Hidden Fees.* Refinancing student loans through LendKey means no origination fees or penalties for making extra or early payments!

## Miscellaneous

### Comprehensive Protection Against Unfair Debt Collection
https://collectionshield360.com

*Credit reporting protection:* On average, we remove 8 out of 10 collection accounts from our client credit reports.

*Statutory damages:* We will seek up to $1,000 compensation from every Debt Collector in violation of FDCPA regulations.

*Cessation of harassment:* We will stop harassing Debt Collector phone calls and mail.

### CourtLinked.com
http://www.courtlinked.com

CourtLinked.com has helped individuals with common legal matters such as Name Changes, Small Claims, Trademarks, and much more!

# What To Do After Your Credit is Fixed

## Little Known Tips And Best Practices

### Credit Line Increases

Once you are approved for a credit card or credit line, regularly ask for a limit increase at least 3 times per year. Credit limit increases are good, and they lower your overall percentage owed on your entire credit profile.

### Business Credit Cards

Get a business credit card. If you do not own a business, you can easily create one at **LegalZoom.com** for less than $200. If you do anything of value outside of your normal 9 to 5 job, even if you sell baked goods and only make a few hundred dollars a year, incorporate a small business, at

least on paper. It will open up many more credit opportunities.

### Charge Cards

Charge cards are better for your credit than regular credit cards. Charge cards are those like American Express, which require you to pay the full balance off every month.

### Hard Inquiries

Inquiries can hurt your score, especially if you apply for several credit cards in a short period of time. However, the same is NOT true with auto loans or home loans. You can apply for as many auto loans or home loans as you want within a 45 day period, and it will all only count as 1 inquiry. (1 for autos and 1 for homes)

### Don't Close Accounts

Do not close any credit cards you have paid off. It looks better to have existing, open accounts with a zero balance. However, to prevent those creditors from closing the account because of non-use, be sure to charge something small every other month, then pay it off.

### Final Notes and Summary

To always keep up to date with our latest and greatest tips & tricks not included in the book, make sure to visit: **http://creditsecret.org/smart-money-club-members**

You will find all sorts of extra juicy tips, dispute letters, videos and more.

Kenneth
October 3, 2016

Follow the book blueprint, be diligent and NEVER except no!!!! GOD BLESSED me with this red hot 2016 Camaro after just 26days in the program!!!! #STAYtheCOURSE

Like    Comment

You, Alison Felix, Brian Barù Murray and 206 others

# Frequently Asked Questions

Over the course of the past few years we have had thousands and thousands of questions, either in our fantastic Smart Money Club Facebook Group or via email to **support@creditsecret.org**

The following pages represent the most common questions. There are many bits of gold in the following pages, and we highly recommend you spend some time reading through all this excellent information.

Remember: if you don't find what you are looking for, feel free to ask your own questions in the group or send us a support request at **support@creditsecret.org**

## Getting Started

**Question:** I'm skeptical. Has anyone really had this work for them?

**Answer:** In our Facebook group there is a search bar. Just do a search for SMCWin and find thousands of posts by members who have taken control of their credit history.

**Question:** I just joined. Where do I start?

**Answer:** When you bought the book, you received a "Welcome Email" with instructions to login to your member dashboard at **http://creditsecret.org/login**. In that dashboard are instructions on how to get started. There is also a video and an audio file of the book in your dashboard. If you cannot locate the welcome email, simply contact **support@creditsecret.org**

**Question:** I just joined. How long before I receive the book?

**Answer:** You get access to the eBook right away in your member dashboard at **http://creditsecret.org/login**. If you ordered a hard copy, it typically takes 3-7 business days. Fulfillment will send you a separate email with tracking information. If you do not get it within this time frame, please send us a note to **support@creditsecret.org**.

**Question:** I just joined. Do I have to wait to receive the book before I can start?

**Answer:** Absolutely not! Sign in to your online dashboard and follow the quickstart instructions!

**Question:** Should I dispute an old <u>paid</u> collection?

**Answer:** First of all you probably should not claim that an item isn't yours if you have paid it, because that is false - unless you paid it by mistake. There are other more ethical ways to get it off, by challenging a reporting error. Second, even paid collections can help your score because if they are several years old they can add to your FICO score in a positive way by counting towards your overall credit age. Sometimes, especially if you have a thin credit file, removing an old paid collection can actually lower your score.

Donna
2 hrs

Thanks to Credit Secrets I was able to purchase my dream vehicle. Once again thank you!!

Love    Comment

You, Steve Solem, Kelly Felix and 72 others

**Question:** My score is X (below 650 with public records and/or collection accounts on your report). Can I start with getting late pays removed?

**Answer:** Yes, you COULD start there, but it will have less impact on your score. Start first with collection accounts and public records because that will have the most impact on your score.

**Question:** How do I get late pays removed?

**Answer:** You can send a goodwill letter from Chapter 2 requesting the removal after you are current for awhile with the account.

**Question:** How do I raise my scores?

**Answer:** Follow every step outlined in this book, without skipping or jumping ahead.

**Question:** What if I've previously used a credit repair firm and one of my items is already marked as "disputed" on my credit report?

**Answer:** You can call the credit bureau(s) and request that the prior dispute(s) be removed. When people apply for a mortgage, the lenders require that no items on their credit report be under dispute, so it is a very common request to have your prior disputes removed. That way you can start the process in our book fresh.

**Question:** Can I dispute an open account I'm tired of paying on?

**Answer:** Sure if you want them to close the account, potentially sue you, AND become a negative listing on your report. This is not a debt eradication system. This system just cleans up your credit report/score. If you want to get rid of a debt you can declare bankruptcy, pay it, or negotiate a debt relief plan with the creditor.

**Question:** There is only a PO Box on my credit report. I can't mail a certified letter to a PO Box. What do I do now?

**Answer:** You can send certified mail to the PO Box. It works for a PO Box the same way it does for you.

Wilfred
December 10 at 5:21am

Started this program in August with a low 500. Now I am on the 700 club except equifax. I am so excited because on Monday I will be closing on our dream house. Brand new house and I didn't put any down payment. This program really works.

Like    Comment

You, Alison Felix, Jeff Lenney and 393 others

They will receive a card in the box saying that they have a letter to sign for. It will be delivered.

**Question:** My letter got returned. Now what?

**Answer:** If you sent the letter to the address reported on your credit report and it got returned, then that proves that the information being reported is inaccurate. In that case you can send a photocopy of the returned envelope and a dispute to the credit bureau for incomplete/inaccurate reporting. That way they will have proof that the address and account is invalid.

**Question:** My creditor sent me papers (an itemized bill or an explanation) but no signature. Now what?

**Answer:** The next step will be sending Part 1, Letter 2.

**Question:** My creditor marked it disputed, but didn't send me proof of a contract with my signature. Now what?

**Answer:** You can send Part 1 Letter 2.

**Question:** My creditor didn't respond at all. Now what?

**Answer:** You can send Part 1 Letter 3.

---

**Question:** My creditor both responded and marked it disputed. Now what?

**Answer:** You can skip to Part 2 letter 1.

---

**Question:** Is there a way to get a judgment, bankruptcy, or other public record removed from my report? If so, how? Who do I send the letter to?

**Answer:** Yes. First you can try sending Part 2 Letter 1 (P2L1) to the credit bureau. If it comes back verified, then refer to Chapter 3 for a special loophole on getting public records removed.

---

**Question:** I was wondering if this can work for student loans?

**Answer:** Many of our members have been successful with removing student loans from their credit report, that are reporting negatively. For this you would use Part 2 Letter 1 in Chapter 2.

**Question:** Where do I get the addresses for my creditors?

**Answer:** Your credit report should list the address of the creditor reporting the line item. If there is no address on your report, you can contact the credit bureau and get it removed for inaccurate or incomplete reporting using the letter from Chapter 2.

---

**Question:** A collection agency is calling us and driving us crazy. Is there anything we can do?

**Answer:** It is generally not a good idea to talk with collection agents on the phone. You can make them stop. Just get the correct mailing address for the agency and write to them using something along these lines:

## Pro Tip: Bad Account Numbers?

If your account number is being reported with X's instead of the full number, this could be considered "inaccurate reporting", and that alone should justify removal. See the letter in Chapter 2 for inaccurate/incomplete reporting.

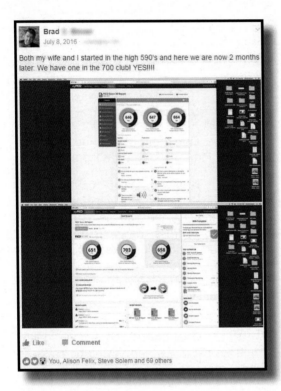

Brad
July 8, 2016

Both my wife and I started in the high 590's and here we are now 2 months later. We have one in the 700 club! YES!!!!

👍 Like    💬 Comment

😊👍❤️ You, Alison Felix, Steve Solem and 69 others

"I require that you communicate with me only in writing, and only at the address provided above. You may not contact me by phone at any time, for any reason." They are required by law (the Fair Debt Collection Practices Act) to honor this written request, and they usually do.

## Credit Reports

**Question:** I'm looking at the credit reports and all my accounts end with 'XXXX' so they are obviously disguising last 4 digits. Do I need to send in my complete account # on my letters? How do I get complete the complete number?

**Answer:** In your letter, include whatever numbers you do know, and then use X's for the remainder like they do. They will be able to identify you by your social security number and/or name & address. They are the ones that reported the information to begin with, it is their job to find it.

---

**Question:** Where should I get my credit report and scores?

**Answer:** Many members are happy with the resource provided at **CreditSecret.org/scores**. Others like to use **www.MyFico.com** or **www.CreditCheckTotal.com** for their reports. And some use Credit Karma or Credit Sesame.

---

**Question:** I have credit monitoring with another service and the scores are way different than what my bank, **MyFico.com**, or other sources say. Why?

**Answer:** Please see Chapter 1 for more about why credit scores fluctuate depending on the provider.

---

**Question:** My FICO score is XXX and a lender turned me down even though it is higher than what they said I needed to get financed. What's going on?

**Answer:** There are 19 different versions of a FICO score. Please see Chapter 1 for more about different scoring models.

---

**Question:** My credit monitoring website only updates once every X days. What do I do if I need to get the latest copy of my report before that?

**Answer:** You can purchase a copy of your report or sign up for monitoring with a second free service.

---

**Question:** How long will it take on average to take it to go from a 500 score to 750?

**Answer:** It depends on you doing things in a timely fashion and following the system exactly. Alison Hilton went from 588 to 781 in 3 months. But she went from 588 to 719 in about 45 days.

---

**Question:** Should I pay off old charge-offs if I can?

**Answer:** If you want to get the most bang for your buck, you should negotiate to pay only if the creditors agree to remove the items from your reports. This is called "pay for deletion." Contact each creditor and say that

you're willing to pay the debt, but only on the condition that the creditor will notify the CRAs to remove the item. Once you get verbal agreement, follow up with each creditor in writing. Before you pay, make sure you get an authorized representative's signature on a letter stating that the creditor agrees to the deletion.

---

**Question:** Are old closed accounts hurting my score? Should I work on getting them removed?

**Answer:** If you closed them, paid them off, and the accounts are in good standing, then they are not doing your credit scores any harm. On the contrary, they may help your average age if they are very old. If the

Crystal
November 30, 2016 ·

I started this program in May. Since my car has 230,000 miles I figured I better get a back up vehicle in case it dies. Well I was approved for a used vehicle which I pick up next week.

👍 Like    💬 Comment

👍❤ You, Alison Felix, Roderick          and 98 others

creditor closed the account because of credit or payment issues, then they are derogatory. In that case you could begin the process with Part 1, Letter 1.

## Sending Letters

**Question:** Will these letters get me in trouble? I'm scared of getting sued!

**Answer:** All we teach is to exercise your rights by demanding that companies prove you actually owe these debts AND that they are being reported fairly and accurately. It has been reported that over 50% of credit reports contain errors or unfair entries. Even if the amount is off 1 dollar, or the date is off one day, your

burden is on THEM to accurately report, not you. These companies are so big and disorganized they literally make MILLIONS of errors or lose/destroy the original paperwork that may or may not have had your signature on it.

With that said, if you want the advice of an attorney, or if you fear being sued or HAVE been sued for some reason, we recommend: **http://creditsecret.org/legalshield**

**Question:** Has anyone had any success getting a specific creditor or collection agency to remove things from their report?

**Answer:** You can use the search bar in the Facebook Group and search for your creditor or collection agencies name. Two of the most popular (or unpopular) are Midland Funding and Portfolio Associates.

**Question:** Is there a letter to get a hard inquiry off of my report?

**Answer:** Yes. Please see Chapter 1.

name is misspelled, and address is wrong, etc - all of these are valid reasons for removal. Why not make them prove it to you? The

**Question:** Do I need to get my old personal information such as addresses or employers removed, or do I send Part 1 Letter 1 first?

**Answer:** That is up to you. Removing your old information is not necessary, but some members have had success with doing it first. The idea is that some of your accounts may be linked to an old address, and once that address is removed, your dispute has a higher probability of success.

**Question:** I have several accounts with one creditor. How many disputes can I put in one letter?

**Answer:** We recommend one dispute, per envelope.

**Question:** Where is the law that requires a signature for it to be a valid debt?

**Answer:** The Fair Credit Reporting Act, Fair Credit Billing Act, and the Fair Debt Collections Act require a signature on an original consumer contract for a debt to be valid.

Dene
November 2, 2016
I followed the books steps this is what I got.

**Question:** When does my 30 day countdown start?

**Answer:** The moment the letter is signed for by the recipient.

**Question:** I received my first response from one of the collection agencies stating that there is no law that obligates them to provide me with signed contracts, copies of state licenses, etc... The letter also said that they requested the credit bureau update my account as "disputed" and that my account was verified, but the proof they provided me was a bill with my SSN, address, and phone number so I'm guessing at this point I should proceed with Part 1 Letter 2?

**Answer:** Yes, you are correct. If things eventually escalate to small claims, which it likely won't, it would be pretty interesting for them to show up without any evidence of your original contract.

---

**Question:** I've been sending out the letters and receiving responses from some and being ignored by others. So I'm at the point where I have no other option but to sue them for false/unfair/unproven reporting. What can I actually sue for? The Credit Reporting agencies are telling me that they legally don't have to send me this stuff. Can I sue the creditors for not sending me proof that I had an agreement with them?

**Answer:** Make sure you read Chapter 4. Use common sense and take the letters you receive with a grain of salt. They may not be entirely accurate or truthful. They may just want you to conform to what's best for them and not you. If you do end up going to court, they'll have their day to explain if they show up. If they are playing hardball, it's more likely that they will take you seriously when they are faced with a court date. Many times they will settle prior to the case, or just not show

up at all. Which means you win by default.

---

**Question:** What if a letter goes unclaimed at the PO box?

**Answer:** Google their physical address and send the letter to them there, via certified mail. Without the signature, it is going to be tough to prove they violated the 30 day rule. Plus it sounds like your future letters will go unanswered at that PO Box address.

---

**Question:** Is it "Game Over" if they provide proof of my signature after the first letter?

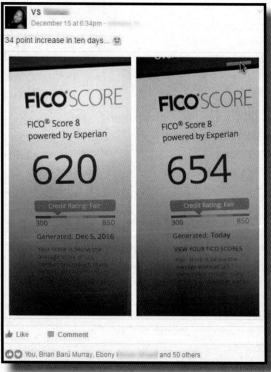

**Question:** If I have 10 items to dispute, can I send 10 letters with 1 dispute per letter all at the same time? Or should I do 1, wait the 31 days, then do another? It could take eons that way, right?

**Answer:** Your goal is to have the highest percentage possible for them to make a mistake. That would mean 10 separate disputes. Clerical errors and your letters getting tossed into a pile, are both your friend.

---

**Question:** Can a Credit Bureau remove a disputed item and then reinsert it later?

**Answer:** Yes. This is a re-insertion. It is very common, and you want to always keep an active eye on your reports.

**Answer:** No because the law states that they need to mark the item as "disputed" regardless. So there is a good chance they will violate the law and not place that notation on your report. Also, you may want to verify that the collector is even licensed to do business in your state AND check to see if they debt is beyond the statute of limitations in your state. If you disagree with what they are claiming you owe, you can still have your day in court.

Here's why this is such a common problem: The CRA has only 30 days after getting a dispute letter to do one of two things: (1) produce evidence that the entry is correct or (2) remove the entry from the report. They don't produce the evidence themselves; they have to get it from the creditor. If they don't hear back from the creditor within the 30-day period, they have no choice

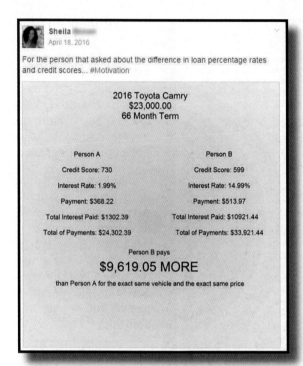

Sheila
April 18, 2016

For the person that asked about the difference in loan percentage rates and credit scores... #Motivation

2016 Toyota Camry
$23,000.00
66 Month Term

| Person A | Person B |
|---|---|
| Credit Score: 730 | Credit Score: 599 |
| Interest Rate: 1.99% | Interest Rate: 14.99% |
| Payment: $368.22 | Payment: $513.97 |
| Total Interest Paid: $1302.39 | Total Interest Paid: $10921.44 |
| Total of Payments: $24,302.39 | Total of Payments: $33,921.44 |

Person B pays

**$9,619.05 MORE**

than Person A for the exact same vehicle and the exact same price

your credit report. See Chapter 7.

---

**Question:** Are your methods legal, or should I check with an attorney?

**Answer:** We are not licensed to give legal advice. We share our information for educational purposes only. What you choose to do is completely up to you. We have seen thousands of members have great success with our program. If you would like to check with a lawyer, we recommend LegalShield **http://creditsecret.org/legalshield**

---

**Question:** Should I get a debt consolidation loan to pay off my credit cards?

**Answer:** If you have a high credit utilization rate (maxing out your cards), then you are hurting your credit scores. A consolidation loan could rectify this. The fact that you paid off all the other cards will not only help your utilization, but probably lower your overall payment and interest rates.

---

but to remove the item. However, sometimes, the evidence arrives a few days or a few weeks later, and it may claim to prove the accuracy of the original entry. Then the Credit Bureau will start reporting it again. The Credit Bureau is supposed to notify you in writing within 5 days if an item is reinserted, but they don't always do it. This is a violation of the FCRA. See Chapter 2 for fighting a re-insertion.

## Miscellaneous

**Question:** What is the shopping cart trick?

A: It is a method of getting credit cards without a hard inquiry on

**Question:** Is it better to pay off credit cards completely or keep a balance?

**Answer:** We have found the sweet spot to be between 10%-30%. So if you have a $1,000 credit line, keeping the balance at $100-$300 would optimize your score.

## Small Claims

**Question:** I filed a small claims lawsuit against a creditor recently. They responded with a motion to move the case from my local county to a US District Court citing that I am alleging violations of the FDCPA and that is a federal law and therefore it should be heard in federal court. Anyone dealt with this?

**Answer:** You can always amend your complaint to include a local state law that is similar to the federal law you are claiming they violated. Please see Chapter 4 for more information on this topic.

**Question:** I received pretty much an entire "book' from a collector with actual proof of signatures etc... but they completely disregarded the fact that I disputed the debt and there is no indication on my report(s) that it's been disputed. So where should I go from this point, wait the thirty days and file suit or should I send another letter?

**Answer:** It is up to you. You can give up and move on to the next account. Or you could send the next letter, letting them know they have violated federal law and that you intend to file a small claims suit. Or you can get even more aggressive and go ahead and file suit. In that case some members have found success by sending them a copy of the lawsuit, and letting them know you are willing to drop it in exchange for them deleting the inaccurate/ unfair information.

**Question:** I've been sued by a collection agency. What should I do?

**Answer:** See our notes on this in Chapter 4.

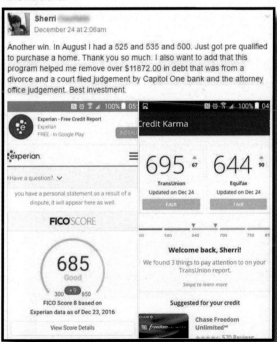

## Bankruptcy and Foreclosure

**Question:** Is this repair method only for removing negative trade lines on the credit report or does it also work for removing things like judgments and bankruptcies as well?

**Answer:** Everything is fair game. For a bankruptcy, you could begin using the system on items that say "included in bankruptcy". And then you could tackle the bankruptcy itself using the information provided in Chapter 3.

---

**Question:** How long will a bankruptcy stay on my reports?

**Answer:** 7 years for completed Chapter 13 bankruptcies and 10 years for Chapter 7 bankruptcies. This period runs from the date the discharge order is entered, not the date the original petition was filed. It's true that most negative items must be removed after seven years, but in the case of Chapter 7 bankruptcies, Congress saw fit to extend the period an extra three years.

---

**Question:** How long will a foreclosure remain on my credit reports?

**Answer:** A foreclosure will remain on your credit report for seven years after the date of the foreclosure sale. As with a bankruptcy, you can challenge an inaccurate, unverifiable, or unfair foreclosure on your reports using the same process as any other derogatory item. And for our loophole regarding these types of accounts you can see Chapter 3.

## Tax Liens and other Public Records

**Question:** For a Tax Lien dispute (Public Record), what is the appropriate strategy?

**Answer:** See our "public record" loophole in Chapter 3.

**Question:** Isn't there a statute of limitations?

**Answer:** Every state has a different statute of limitations for certain debts and public records. You can check yours in Statute of Limitations Chart near the end of this book.

---

**Question:** Can the system be used for credit card companies that have won a judgment against me? Is it still the same process starting with the letters to the original creditor? Does the fact that they went to court and got the judgment change what they need to provide me with if requested?

**Answer:** You actually can dispute a judgment directly with the credit bureaus using Part 2, Letter 1, not the court itself. Be sure to check our loophole on public records like judgments in Chapter 3

---

## Credit Cards

**Question:** Should I close the credit card accounts I don't use?

**Answer:** We don't recommend closing unused credit card accounts. From the point of view of getting your scores as high as possible, it's better to keep these accounts open, even though you don't use them. This all has to do with the utilization ratio. The more open cards you have (within reason) with balances below 30 percent of the credit limit, the better.

When you close down an account, you no longer have it available, and it no longer counts in calculating your utilization ratio.

**Question:** Will a Goodwill Letter work with several late pays on one account?

**Answer:** You can certainly give it a try. See Chapter 2 for the Goodwill letter. Another option would be to dispute/challenge it with Part 1, Letter 1 if you don't agree with it.

---

**Question:** Should I send a Goodwill Letter certified, return receipt requested?

**Answer:** No, there is no need to do this. Stick them in an envelope and send them regular mail. Some members also fax them with success.

---

**Question:** I sent a Goodwill Letter and it didn't work. The creditor responded that "they are unable to update any information that was reported correctly."

**Answer:** You have a few options. Because the majority of these companies are so big, there is a good chance you could try again, reaching a different person that might very well help you out. If that fails, then you could dispute the late pays by starting the process with Part 1, Letter 1. If that fails, then skip to Part 2, Letter 1, and dispute the information with the Credit Bureaus.

# Statute of Limitations Chart

A debt collector no longer has a right to sue for payment, once a debt ages past the statute of limitations, or SOL, on a state by state basis.

If a debt collector tries to take to you to court for a debt past the SOL, then they are in violation of the Fair Debt Collection Practices Act

That chart below shows each state's SOL for delinquent debt.

| State | Written contracts | Oral contracts | Promissory notes | Open-ended accounts (including credit cards) |
|---|---|---|---|---|
| Alabama | 3 | 6 | 6 | 3 |
| Alaska | 3 | 6 | 3 | 3 |
| Arizona | 6 | 3 | 5 | 3 |
| Arkansas | 5 | 3 | 3 | 5 |
| California | 4 | 2 | 4 | 4 |
| Colorado | 6 | 6 | 6 | 6 |
| Connecticut | 6 | 3 | 6 | 6 |
| Delaware | 3 | 3 | 3 | 3 |
| D.C. | 3 | 3 | 3 | 3 |
| Florida | 5 | 4 | 5 | 4 |
| Georgia | 6 | 4 | 6 | 4 or 6** |
| Hawaii | 6 | 6 | 6 | 6 |
| Idaho | 5 | 4 | 5 | 5 |
| Illinois | 10 | 5 | 10 | 5 or 10*** |
| Indiana | 10 | 6 | 10 | 6 |
| Iowa | 10 | 5 | 5 | 10 |
| Kansas | 3 | 3 | 3 | 3 |
| Kentucky | 15 | 5 | 15 | 5 or 15**** |
| Louisiana | 3 | 10 | 10 | 3 |
| Maine | 6 | 6 | 6 | 6 |
| Maryland | 3 | 3 | 6 | 3 |
| Massachusetts | 6 | 6 | 6 | 6 |
| Michigan | 6 | 6 | 6 | 6 |
| Minnesota | 6 | 6 | 6 | 6 |
| Mississippi | 3 | 3 | 3 | 3 |

| State | Written contracts | Oral contracts | Promissory notes | Open-ended accounts (including credit cards) |
|---|---|---|---|---|
| Missouri | 5 | 5 | 5 | 5 |
| Montana | 8 | 5 | 8 | 8 |
| Nebraska | 4 | 4 | 4 | 4 |
| Nevada | 4 | 4 | 4 | 4 |
| New Hampshire | 3 | 3 | 3 | 3 |
| New Jersey | 6 | 6 | 6 | 6 |
| New Mexico | 4 | 4 | 4 | 4 |
| New York | 6 | 6 | 6 | 6 |
| North Carolina | 3 | 3 | 5 | 3 |
| North Dakota | 6 | 6 | 6 | 6 |
| Ohio | 6 | 6 | 6 | 6 |
| Oklahoma | 5 | 3 | 5 | 3 or 5**** |
| Oregon | 6 | 6 | 6 | 6 |
| Pennyslvania | 4 | 4 | 4 | 4 |
| Rhode Island | 10 | 10 | 10 | 10 |
| South Carolina | 10 | 10 | 3 | 3 |
| South Dakota | 6 | 3 | 6 | 6 |
| Tennessee | 6 | 6 | 6 | 6 |
| Texas | 4 | 4 | 4 | 4 |
| Utah | 6 | 4 | 6 | 4 |
| Vermont | 5 | 3 | 6 | 3 |
| Virginia | 6 | 6 | 5 | 6 |
| Washington | 6 | 3 | 6 | 6 |
| West Virginia | 10 | 10 | 10 | 10 |
| Wisconsin | 6 | 6 | 10 | 6 |
| Wyoming | 10 | 8 | 10 | 8 |

** Georgia Court of Appeals came out with a decision on January 24, 2008 in Hill v. American Express that in Georgia the statute of limitations on a credit card is six years after the amount becomes due and payable.

*** An Illinois appeals court ruled on May 20, 2009, that the statute of limitations on a credit card debt without a written contract was 5 years.

**** State law doesn't specify the limitations on open accounts.

# Glossary

### Account

An account represents a relationship between a company (the account owner) and consumer, where the consumer purchases a product or service in such a way that represents the transfer of money over time.

### Account Holder

The person(s) and or guarantor(s) in whose name an Account was established; the person or entity who or which is obligated to repay an Account, or if there are multiple persons or entities obligated to repay an Account, all such persons or entities collectively; the obligor or obligors on an Account.

### Account Reviews

Inquiries made into a consumer's credit history by creditors, with whom the consumer has a current relationship.

### Adjustable Rate Mortgage (ARM)

A mortgage where the interest rate fluctuates over the life of the loan.

### Adverse Action

An unfavorable action, such as the denial of credit, insurance or employment, taken by a creditor or other entity, affecting a consumer. Under the Fair Credit Reporting Act (FCRA), creditors must disclose the reasons for any adverse action.

### Annual Fee

The yearly fee charged by a lender to maintain an account.

### Annual Percentage Rate (APR)

The cost of credit at a yearly rate.

### Balance Transfer

Moving your balance from one credit card to another to take advantage of features the new card offers.

### Balance

The amount of money that you owe to a particular lender.

### Bank Card

A credit card issued through a bank.

### Bankruptcy

A legal proceeding that relieves you of the responsibility of paying your debts or provides you with protection while attempting to repay your debts.

### Bankruptcy Discharge

The release, by the Bankruptcy Court, of the debtor from all of his dischargeable debts, whether then payable or not. A permanent injunction against any collection action for pre–filing dischargeable debts. The goal a debtor seeks when filing for bankruptcy protection.

## Bankruptcy Dismissed

An order by the Bankruptcy Court terminating a specific bankruptcy case. Creditors may resume collection efforts upon dismissal of the debtor's case.

## Better Business Bureau

The BBB serves as an intermediary between consumers and businesses, handling consumer disputes against businesses. The Better Business Bureau is not affiliated with any governmental agency.

## Chapter 7 Bankruptcy

The chapter of the Bankruptcy Code that provides for court-administered liquidation of the assets of a financially troubled individual or business.

## Chapter 11 Bankruptcy

The chapter of the Bankruptcy Code that is usually used for the reorganization of a financially troubled business. Used as an alternative to liquidation under Chapter 7.

## Chapter 13 Bankruptcy

The chapter of the Bankruptcy Code in which debtors repay debts according to a plan accepted by the debtor, the creditors, and the court.

## Charge Card

A credit card that requires full payment of the bill each month; no interest is charged. The American Express Card is an example.

## Charge-Off

A loan or credit card debt written off as uncollectible from the borrower. The debt, however, remains valid and subject to collection.

## ChexSystems

ChexSystems is a check verification service and consumer credit reporting agency owned by the eFunds subsidiary of Fidelity National Information Services. It provides information about the use of deposit accounts by consumers.

## Closed by Grantor

A credit account that has been closed at the grantor's request wherein a creditor cancels your charge privileges.

## Collection

When a borrower falls behind, the lender contacts them in an effort to bring the loan current. The loan goes to "collection."

## Consumer

A "consumer" is defined as an individual.

## Consumer Report

A "consumer report" is any written, oral, or other communication of any information by a Consumer reporting agency that bears on a consumer's creditworthiness, credit standing, Credit capacity, character, general reputation, personal characteristics, or mode of living which is used or expected to be used or collected, in whole or in part, for the purpose of Serving as a factor in establishing the consumer's eligibility for:

1. Credit or insurance to be used primarily for personal, family, or household purposes

2. Employment purposes; or any other purpose authorized under section 604 (15 U.S.C. § 1681b).

## Consumer Reporting Agency (CRA)

An agency that is a clearinghouse for information on the credit payment history of individuals or firms. There are three major credit bureaus, Equifax, Experian and TransUnion, and they are regulated by the federal Fair Credit Reporting Act (FCRA).

## Consumer Financial Protection Bureau

The Consumer Financial Protection Bureau (CFPB) is an agency of the United States government responsible for consumer protection in the financial sector. CFPB jurisdiction includes banks, credit unions, securities firms, payday lenders, mortgage-servicing operations, foreclosure relief services, debt collectors and other financial companies operating in the United States.

## Credit

A trust or promise to buy now and pay later under designated terms for goods or services.

## Credit Card

A card that allows a consumer to pay a portion or all of the outstanding amount each month and has a credit limit. Visa, MasterCard, and Discover are examples.

## Credit Check

An inquiry to confirm a consumer's credit payment history.

## Credit Fraud

A case when someone has stolen a consumer's identity by fraudulently using that consumer's social security number or other personal information to acquire credit in his or her name.

## Credit Dispute

To request an investigation of the accuracy of information on a credit report.

## Credit File

The collection of information each of the credit reporting agencies maintains in their databases.

## Credit History

The record of a consumer's credit accounts and manner of payment (MOP). Credit history includes high credit, current balance, credit limit, and 24 months or more of MOP history.

## Credit Inquiries

Credit inquiries are a notation listed on your credit report that a lender has checked your credit file. "Hard" inquiries can impact your Credit Score, while "soft" ones don't. Creditors see only your "Hard" inquiries.

## Credit Limit

The maximum amount you are allowed to borrow from a lender under the terms of your agreement for an account.

## Credit Monitoring Service

Services that monitor activity in your credit file and alert you to key changes in your file.

## Credit Repair

Credit repair is a general term used to describe the practice of improving or rehabilitating one's financial reputation (creditworthiness) with creditors.

## Credit Report

A record of the information in your financial credit file that is used by a lender, employer, or others to help evaluate you when you apply for a loan, job or in certain other circumstances.

## Credit Risk

An assessment of a consumer's likelihood of fulfilling the terms of a credit agreement.

## Credit Score

A credit score is a numerical index which represents an estimate of an individual's financial creditworthiness. It is based on a subset of the information in an individual's credit report.

## Creditor

Person or business to whom a debt is owed.

## Creditworthiness

An assessment of a consumer's past credit behavior that allows a potential lender to decide whether or not to extend credit. Credit reporting agencies are private, for-profit companies that collect and sell information about a person's credit history. Typical clients include banks, mortgage lenders and credit card companies that use the information to screen applicants for loans and credit cards.

## Current Balance

(a) the unpaid balance for each account;

(b) the Account balance, which does not include any finance or late charges assessed after Charge–off Date.

## Date Closed

The date when a credit agreement or account was terminated.

**Date Opened**

The date when a credit agreement or account was established.

**Date of Last Activity (DOLA)**

The date when one of three things happens on any active account: the consumer makes a payment, misses a payment, or the balance of the account increases

**Debt Consolidation**

Debt consolidation entails taking out one loan to pay off many others. This is often done to secure a lower interest rate, secure a fixed interest rate or for the convenience of servicing only one loan.

**Debt Settlement**

A process to reduce or pay off old debt by negotiating a lower amount due with the creditor.

**Debt-to-Income Ratio**

Your income compared to the debt you owe.

**Default**

Failure to fulfill an agreed-upon financial obligation, such as making a loan payment.

**Delinquency**

Past-due payment on a loan.

**Dispute**

If you have reviewed your credit report and found some data to be inaccurate, you can contact the companies involved to have it investigated and/or removed. This is considered a dispute.

**Fair and Accurate Credit Transactions Act (FACTA)**

A federal law that amended the federal Fair Credit Reporting Act in many areas. The law provided, among other things, additional protections for consumers in connection with the prevention and remediation of identity theft and the accuracy of credit reports. It includes your right to a free copy of your credit report from each of the three major credit reporting agencies every 12 months, which must be requested through the centralized source established under the FACT Act.

**Fair Credit Billing Act (FCBA)**

This Act, amending the Truth in Lending Act, requires prompt written acknowledgment of consumer billing complaints and investigation of billing errors by creditors. The amendment prohibits creditors from taking actions that adversely affect the consumer's credit standing until an investigation is completed, and affords other protection during disputes. The amendment also requires that creditors promptly post payments to the consumer's account, and either refund overpayments or credit them to the consumer's account

## Fair Credit Reporting Act (FCRA)

Fair Credit Reporting Act (effective April 25, 1971) is part of a group of acts in the Federal Consumer Credit Protection Act. The Act protects information collected by consumer reporting agencies such as credit bureaus, medical information companies and tenant screening services. Information in a consumer report cannot be provided to anyone who does not have a purpose specified in the Act. Companies that provide information to consumer reporting agencies also have specific legal obligations, including the duty to investigate disputed information. Also, users of the information for credit, insurance, or employment purposes must notify the consumer when an adverse action is taken on the basis of such reports. Further, users must identify the company that provided the report, so that the accuracy and completeness of the report may be verified or contested by the consumer.

## Fair Debt Collection Practices Act (FDCPA)

Under this Act (Title VIII of the Consumer Credit Protection Act), third-party debt collectors are prohibited from employing deceptive or abusive conduct in the collection of consumer debts incurred for personal, family, or household purposes. Such collectors may not, for example, contact debtors at odd hours, subject them to repeated telephone calls, threaten legal action that is not actually contemplated, or reveal to other persons the existence of debts.

## Federal Trade Commission (FTC)

A federal agency whose duty is to investigate unfair methods of competition in business, fraudulent advertising, etc., and to restrain or prosecute those charged with such practices. The Commission's primary purpose is to protect consumers.

## FICO® Score

A FICO® score is a credit score produced from models developed by Fair Isaac Corporation. The score is used to measure a consumer's creditworthiness and risk, and is in use worldwide. FICO® scores range from 300 - 850 and are available through all of the major consumer reporting agencies in the United States: Equifax, Experian, and TransUnion. (FICO® is a registered trademark of Fair Isaac Corporation).

## Finance Charges

The amount you are charged to use credit.

## Fixed-Rate Mortgage

A mortgage where the interest rate of the loan remains the same over the life of the loan.

**Foreclosure**

The legal process by which a lender, usually a bank or other financial institution, acquires real property because the borrower failed to pay the mortgage.

**Freeze**

Also known as a security freeze, you restrict access to your credit report, which in turn makes it more difficult for creditors to see your credit report.

**Furnishers**

Any company that submits information about you to be included on your credit report.

**Garnishment**

A legal process whereby a lender who has obtained a judgment on a debt can receive full or partial payment by seizure of a portion of the debtor's assets (wages, bank account, etc.).

**Grace Period**

The number of days between a statement due date and the payment due date during which you do not incur finance charges.

**Gross Monthly Income**

What you earn before taxes are deducted.

**HIPAA**

HIPAA is the acronym for the Health Insurance Portability and Accountability Act that was passed by Congress in 1996. HIPAA Mandates industry-wide standards for health care information on electronic billing and other processes; and requires the protection and confidential handling of protected health information.

**Identity Confirmation**

The successful verification of a consumer's identity.

**Identity Theft / Identity Fraud**

A crime that involves using another's name, Social Security Number or other personal information to acquire credit, make purchases or commit a crime in that name.

**Inquiry**

An examination of a consumer's credit history. When your credit report is made available to another party, such as a lender, landlord or insurer.

**Installment Loan**

A credit account in which the amount of the payment and the number of payments are predetermined or fixed.

**Interest**

The cost of borrowing or lending money, usually a percentage of the amount borrowed or loaned.

## Interest Rate

A percentage of money charged by a lender, for borrowing money. For example, you might get charged 12.5% interest on any credit card balance carried over, or you might qualify for a 4.5% car loan.

## Judgment

A final court ruling resolving the key questions in a lawsuit and determining the rights and obligations of the opposing parties.

## Last Contact Date

The date when the debtor or the debtor's legal representative last responded, either by a written or verbal response, to debt collection action.

## Late Fee

A fee attached to a delinquent account.

## Late Payment

A delinquent payment; a failure to deliver a loan or debt payment on or before the time agreed. Late payments are reported to the credit bureaus by creditors, and appear as negative items on your credit reports.

## LexisNexis

LexisNexis (which acquired ChoicePoint) is the largest data-broker in the world and reseller of credit information. As of 2006, the company has the world's largest electronic database for legal and public-records related information.

## Lien

A legal claim upon real estate or personal property for the satisfaction of a debt. Liens you agree to are called security interests, and include mortgages, home equity loans, car loans and personal loans for which you pledge property to guarantee repayment. Liens created without your consent are called non consensual liens, and include judgment liens (liens filed by a creditor who has sued you and obtained a judgment), tax liens and mechanic's liens (liens filed by a contractor who worked on your house but wasn't paid).

## Line of Credit

Credit limit established by a creditor

## Metro 2

Metro 2 is a data specification created by the Consumer Data Industry Association for credit reporting data furnishers (who are members of the credit bureau with a data furnishing service agreement) to report consumers' credit history information to major credit bureaus electronically and in a standardized format.

## Open account

An account that is active or still being paid.

### Paid as agreed

A designation on the credit report that indicates the consumer is repaying the credit account according to the terms of the credit agreement.

### Permissible Purpose

As defined in 604 of the Fair Credit Reporting Act (FCRA), only specific reasons for requesting a credit report are deemed "permissible." Requests not meeting this criteria must be denied.

### Principal

The outstanding balance of a loan, exclusive of interest and other charges.

### Points

Fees paid to a lender for a loan. They are often linked to the interest rate and are generally used to lower the interest rate of the loan.

### Preapproval

When a mortgage lender reviews your credit and commits to a specific loan amount.

### Prequalification

When a mortgage lender reviews your credit history, income, assets and liabilities in order to determine an appropriate loan amount.

### Principal Balance

Defined as account principal and other legally collectible costs, expenses, and interest accrued prior to the Charge–off Date, less payments or settlements since charge off, if any.

### Public Record

Information obtained from court records about such things as state or federal tax liens, bankruptcy filings and judgments against you in civil actions. Public records are open to any person who requests them.

### Reaged Account

An account that is brought to a current status, even though the total past due amount has not been paid. Some unscrupulous companies may do this in order to start the Date of Last Activity over again, in an effort to reset the typical 7 year clock for a negative item to automatically fall off of your credit report.

### Repossession

The action taken (usually by a financial institution) to recover an object that was used as collateral, rented or leased in a transaction.

### Revolving Balance

The total balance of all revolving credit accounts.

### Revolving Charge Account

Credit automatically available up to a predetermined limit so long as a consumer makes regular payments.

## Revolving Credit

An account that requires at least a specified minimum payment each month plus a service charge on the balance, which can fluctuate up to the credit limit. As the balance declines, the amount of the service charge, or interest, also declines.

## Secured Credit Card

A credit card secured by a savings account.

## Settled In Full

The Debtor has satisfied the Account obligation with full payment of the amount due.

## Settlement

(a)    payment of the adjustment amount of an account, including principal, interest and fees;

(b)    a    copy    of    a    written settlement    agreement    or    other written documentation evidencing a settlement.

## Small Claims Court

Small claims court is a special court where disputes are resolved quickly and inexpensively. In small claims court, the rules are simplified and the hearing is informal. Attorneys are generally not allowed. The person who files the claim is called the plaintiff.

## State Attorney General

The attorney general is an executive office in all 50 states that serves as the chief legal advisor and chief law enforcement officer for the state government and is empowered to prosecute violations of state law, represent the state in legal disputes and issue legal advice to state agencies and the legislature.

## Tax Lien

A charge upon real or personal property for the satisfaction of debts related to taxes.

## Term

The amount of time in which a loan must be repaid in full.

## Variable Rate

A variable rate is an interest rate that may fluctuate over the life of a loan, typically in response to changes in the interest rate marketplace.

## VantageScore®

First announced in March 2006, VantageScore® is the latest addition in consumer credit scoring models. Its methodologies and algorithms were cooperatively developed by the three major consumer reporting agencies: Equifax, Experian, and TransUnion. VantageScores® range from 501 - 900.

# Identity Theft and How to Protect Yourself

As you may have heard at some point, Equifax had a giant cybersecurity breach occur between mid-May and July of 2017, which compromised the personal information of as many as 143 million Americans — almost half the country. Cybercriminals accessed sensitive information -- including names, social security numbers, birth dates, addresses, and the numbers of some driver's licenses. Equifax even admitted that credit card numbers for about 209,000 U.S. customers were exposed, as was "personal identifying information" belonging to roughly 182,000 U.S. customers involved in credit report disputes.

Unlike other data breaches, not all of the people affected by the Equifax breach may be aware that they're customers of the company. Equifax gets its data from credit card companies, banks, retailers, and lenders who report on the credit activity of individuals to credit reporting agencies, as well as by purchasing public records.

Obviously, this is very bad news. It's also one of the top reasons to make sure you always monitor your credit reports, bank statements, and credit card statements. The hackers hang on to this information for a long time as well, so never think that enough time has passed that you can't be affected. They can pounce at any time.

## Take These Steps to Protect Yourself From Identity Theft

1. Review your credit report at least once a year to be certain that it doesn't include accounts that you have not opened. If you don't already have it, sign up for credit monitoring. creditsecret.org/scores

2. Be sure to secure your social security number (SSN). Never carry your social security card in your wallet or write your number on your checks.

3. Don't respond to unsolicited requests for personal information (your name, birthdate, social security number, or bank account number) by phone, email, or online.

4. Request a freeze of your credit reports from all three credit bureaus.

5. Never leave mail pile up in your mailbox. Always place a hold when you are away from home for several days.

6. Use the built-in security features on mobile devices, especially if you have contacts, banking websites and applications saved.

7. Always use updated firewall settings when on a public wi-fi network. Consider using a virtual private network, which can give you the privacy of secured private network.

8. Regularly review your credit card and bank account statements looking for unauthorized transactions.

9. Shred receipts, credit offers, account statements, and expired credit cards, to prevent "dumpster divers" from getting your personal information.

10. Store personal information in a safe place at home and work.

11. Create and use complex passwords that hackers cannot guess. Always change your password if a company that you do business with has a security breach of its online resources.

12. Federal laws require credit card companies to have consumer protections in place, and they have dedicated fraud departments to investigate all claims. This is one of the reasons you always want to use a credit card for online purchases versus a debit card.

## Recovering From Identity Theft

First, you will need to figure out what kind of fraud has occurred. If you see an error on a credit card statement or financial account, you'll need to contact that company to report it and possibly file a claim.

If you believe fraud has occurred, the FTC recommends that you place a fraud alert with one of the three major credit reporting agencies. They are, by Federal Law, required to report the fraud alert to the other two agencies.

The alert automatically entitles you to a free copy of your credit report. Review your credit report for any accounts you did not open, or activity you did not conduct, and confirm that the report has your correct name, address and Social Security number.

Next, you will want to file a complaint form with the trade commission and an identity theft report with your local police department. Be sure to make multiple copies of these reports and file the originals safely away. Typically, identity theft is difficult to prosecute, but these documents can be helpful to the credit agencies and the financial institutions you do business with.

The first fraud alert is, for example, if you lose your wallet. That requires potential creditors to take certain steps to verify your identity before opening new accounts in your name. The next kind of alert is an extended fraud alert. The extended fraud alert lasts seven years and will require any creditor to contact you personally before any new accounts are opened.

## Credit Freezes

One of the other precautions you can take is to put a freeze on your credit report. By putting a freeze on your credit report, businesses and creditors cannot check your credit history unless you temporarily lift the freeze. The costs and rules vary state by state, so be sure to check with the credit bureaus for your specific steps.

### Equifax Credit Freeze:

https://www.freeze.equifax.com

### TransUnion Credit Freeze:

https://www.transUnion.com/credit-freeze/place-credit-freeze

### Experian Credit Freeze:

https://www.experian.com/freeze/center.html

## Contacting Your Credit Companies

Be careful when dealing with the companies that have your accounts that have been affected. You don't want to just close accounts as that may negatively affect your credit scores. Inform the creditor that you have reason to suspect you are a victim of fraud and ask it for the company's policy in situations like these.

Sometimes, the creditor will simply assign you a new account number, such as a credit card that might have been compromised. They will shut off the current card, and simply issue you a new one with a new number.

Whatever choices you make, always make sure to document every person you speak to, the date and time you spoke with them, and the request you made. You may need this for any future interactions about your account.